CHURCH POLITY

International Studies in Protestant Church Polity

The Journal of the Society for Protestant Church Polity

ISSN 2693-2970 (Print)
ISSN 2963-2989 (Online)

Volume 2, Number 1
Autumn 2021

Church Polity

Church Polity: International Studies in Protestant Church Polity is a peer-reviewed international journal of church polity from and for the Protestant world. The journal provides a forum for discussion on matters of church polity across denominational and national boundaries. Contributions are welcomed for a variety of approaches that provide for historical, theological, biblical, and legal analyses of church polity topics from around the Protestant world. *Church Polity* originates from the Society for Protestant Church Polity, an international network of church polity scholars and practitioners.

Contents

Church Polity (ISSN 2693-2970 (Print); ISSN 2963-2989 (Online)) is published annually by the Society for Protestant Church Polity in partnership with the Beardslee Press.

ISBN: 978-1-7327952-2-8

Editorial Introduction

Klaas-Willem de Jong
Matthew J. van Maastricht

When we launched *Church Polity: International Studies in Protestant Church Polity*, we would not have imagined that we would still be in the midst of the COVID-19 pandemic for a second issue. As with the first issue, the pressures from the pandemic have impacted this issue, as well. We are grateful for the authors who, in spite of the additional challenges and pressures that abound in this season, submitted articles and reviewed books. A journal is not possible without contributions, and we are pleased to offer a second issue.

This second issue includes contributions from authors of different denominations—different traditions—each in different contexts. And yet, even with these various contexts, there are often remarkable points of contact, and so although each of these are rooted in their own context, the value of the contributions is not contextually bound, that is, they provide us a window to consider the churches, the nations, the cultures, the contexts in which we each find ourselves.

Kathleen Smith provides the first contribution and reflects upon church polity developments in the Christian Reformed Church in North America (CRC) over the past quarter century. The themes that she touches on are common to many churches: declining membership numbers, women in ecclesiastical office, sacramental tensions, human sexuality, and ecumenism. In her contribution, she presents a denomination that has sought to navigate the (at times, at least) tension between fidelity to tradition while at the same time being responsive to the needs of the particular context.

From the United States, we move to Indonesia, where Vera Loupatty offers an interesting contribution which helps to reframe the relationship between church and state as not one of power, status, privilege, or benefits, but rather on vulnerability. As she notes, there have been a significant number of periods where the church and state relationship is based on competition for superiority (i.e., does the church dominate over the state, or the state over the church?). Rather than this, the church is called to a friendly relationship with the state rooted in mutual service for the good of the world, rather than focusing on the mutual benefits of church and state, or in the competition to dominate one over the other. In both of these scenarios the focus is on the institutional success—centered in profit or power, rather than that of the good of the world. In this, she reflects on the church order of her own church, The Christian Evangelical Church in Minahasa, and historical (particularly colonial) relationship between the church and the state, how this has influenced the current church order, and how it might be re-envisioned. In a world where power, prestige, profit, and luxury is still a significant driving force, this contribution will certainly invite readers of a variety of contexts to reflect on this.

And finally, from Austrailia, Mark Vainikka and Luke van der Laan offer an essay rooted in the reality of the Lutheran Church of Australia (LCA). The LCA finds itself in a similar position to many churches in different places in the world of a shrinking membership, but with a ministry need that continues to grow. That is, at the same time that the membership of the LCA decreases, its aged-care, service, and educational agencies continue to grow. This, of course, invites questions of identity: that is, is the LCA primilarily a church with agencies to further its mission work, or is it primarily an organization of social service agencies that also has a shrinking church attached? Vainikka and Van der Laan reflect on this identity question in light of Lutheran ecclesiology and the way in which Lutheran polity is able to adapt to the changing environment in which the LCA finds itself. In doing so, they provide some important points of consideration to ensure that the work of the LCA maintains consistent with Lutheran ecclesiology and polity. As with other contributions, this essay is rooted in the experience of the LCA, but it also invites us to reflect on similar considerations in our own churches in our own contexts.

Finally, we are happy to bring reviews of two recently published books in the church polity discipline. The first is a review essay which not only considers the particular volume at hand, but also bigger picture considerations within the discipline itself. The second is a review of a dissertation recently published on interfaith marriage in Indonesia, which, as you will see, has meaning for a broader readership than simply Indonesians.

This journal originates from the Society for Protestant Church Polity, an international society of church polity scholars and practitioners whose membership currently spans seventeen countries across five continents. To find out more about the Society, including information about membership, submission guidelines, and issues of Church Polity please visit http://churchpolity.org. We also wish to express gratitude to the Beardslee Press at New Brunswick Theological Seminary for being willing to partner with us on this venture.

Church Polity: International Studies in Protestant Church Polity
Autumn 2021 2(1), pp. 1–16

Reflections on Church Polity in the Past Twenty-five Years in the Christian Reformed Church in North America

Kathleen S. Smith

Church polity in the Christian Reformed Church in North America (CRCNA) has gone through many changes in the past twenty-five years, and those changes have required the denomination to balance tensions and allow for differences within and between its churches. Unity in the church is always desired, but the CRCNA has recognized that unity does not always need to mean uniformity. The changes of the past quarter century can be seen in three major trends: 1) changes in synodical decisions on ethical and doctrinal matters, 2) changes in approaches to ecumenical activities, and 3) changes in the understanding of church offices, especially that of commissioned pastors and deacons. All three areas show a denomination that is working to balance tensions while maintaining the principles of its polity. Within the first trend, four church polity

---

Kathleen S. Smith is the Adjunct Professor Church Polity at Calvin Theological Seminary and the Associate Director of the Calvin Institute for Christian Worship at Calvin University. Corresponding Author email: kss4@calvinseminary.edu case studies are considered regarding women in ecclesiastical office, paedocommunion, infant baptism vs. infant dedication, and human sexuality. These case studies demonstrate how the CRCNA has processed change on significant issues, including those that are understood as confessional interpretations, church order matters, and pastoral advice to the churches. All of these changes and trends over the past twenty-five years—changes in doctrinal and ethical positions, in approaches to ecumenical relationships, and in the offices of the church—indicate a denomination that seeks to be true to its roots and the principles of its polity, while also adjusting to changing times and the need for greater flexibility as it continues to contextualize its mission and ministry in North America.

Introduction

A quarter of a century is a significant amount of time in the life of the church, a span in which much change can occur. Often church polity is considered an area of church life that is especially slow to change, but it has demonstrated otherwise in recent years in North America.

Since 1995 there have been many changes in church polity in North America generally, and many specific changes in the polity of the CRCNA, some of which are explored in this essay. But while the changes identified in this essay relate to issues that have been common in many Reformed churches and other Christian denominations as well during the past twenty-five years, the way they have played out in the polity of the CRCNA may be unique.

Three areas of change in CRCNA polity will be described in this essay: 1) changes in synodical decisions on ethical and doctrinal matters, 2) changes in approaches to ecumenical activities, and 3) changes in understanding of church offices, especially that of commissioned pastors and deacons. All three areas show a denomination that is working to balance tensions while maintaining the principles of its polity.

Changes in Synodical Decisions on Ethical and Doctrinal Matters

The CRCNA has a history of studying issues carefully and thoughtfully and producing nuanced positions that often have allowed for differences in the level of authority and agreement expected, and also differences in methods of implementation. Synodical study committees have produced a list of "position statements" that can be found on the denominational website,[1] a list that has grown in recent years. The positions vary greatly in scope and in the type of decision the synod (denominational assembly) has adopted—for instance, a confessional interpretation, an instruction, a recommendation or encouragement, or pastoral guidance or advice. The Position Statements website also cites a synodical report from 1975 on the relationship of those different types of synodical decisions to our Reformed confessions.[2] That synodical report acknowledged both that synodical decisions are "settled and binding, unless proved to be in conflict with the Word of God or the Church Order,"[3] and that "there is an obvious difference between the use and function of a pronouncement as interpretation of the confessions and a decision involving 'guidelines' or 'pastoral advice.' It is the wording of synod's decision which usually indicates the precise character of its decision, and this wording of the decision determines its use and function." Further, the report said that "no synodical decision involving doctrinal or ethical pronouncements is to be considered on a par with the confessions."[4] So, when considering synodical decisions in the CRCNA, one needs to carefully review the position and the wording of synod's decisions to understand the scope and intent of the position, and how a church or individual in the CRC would abide by it, as required by the Church Order.

In addition to an increase in decisions that are considered positions on ethical issues, a noticeable trend in the past twenty-five years is that the CRCNA synod has made decisions and taken positions on a number of issues, but has allowed churches and regional classes to implement those decisions in various ways that are suitable for their context. Whether this trend is motivated by compromise or collaboration is not

1 https://www.crcna.org/welcome/beliefs/position-statements.

2 Report 47, "Synodical Decisions and the Confessions," *Agenda for Synod 1975*, 595-604.

3 Article 29, *Church Order and Its Supplements, 2020.*

4 Report 47, "Synodical Decisions and the Confessions," *Agenda for Synod 1975*, 598.

always easy to determine, but there have been arguments for these decisions that call for maintaining unity in the church and getting on with the mission and ministry of the church, rather than engaging in endless debates on controversial topics and votes that sometimes go back and forth year after year. In other words, when consensus cannot be reached, in recent years the CRCNA has tended to allow for different viewpoints and different practices in regional classes and local congregations. The synod's role has increasingly become that of allowing for change but also allowing the regional classes and local church councils (governing bodies) and consistories (elders) to decide how to implement those decisions in ways that are fitting to the local contexts and convictions. The result has been that synod allows for more progressive perspectives and practices while protecting the consciences of those who prefer to hold to more traditional views. This allows the churches to continue to work together and recognizes that on many, if not most, issues there is a lot of agreement, but where strong convictions are held that could threaten to divide the denomination, different views can be respected for the sake of unity. That unity is not easy to achieve or to hold, but so far, the value of continuing to stay together has outweighed the differences that might tear the church apart.

Balancing Tensions in an Age of Declining Numbers

Living in the tension and balancing those tensions is not easy, and often leads to energized discussions where proponents on both sides of an issue are stretched to maintain respect for those with whom they differ. And, of course, some are not able to live in the tension and opt out over contentious issues. The CRCNA has declined in numbers of churches and members over the past twenty-five years as well, from 74,278 families and 294,179 members in 1995, to 68,402 families and 216,336 members in 2020. In 2021, the CRCNA statistics show 66,885 families and 211,706 members.[5] Some of that decline may be due to people leaving over various issues—either impatient that the CRCNA is not making progress

[5] https://www.crcna.org/sites/default/files/membership_stats_2021.pdf

on issues such as diversity and inclusion or concerned that the CRCNA is moving too fast on social issues and losing its doctrinal moorings in the process. But the decline may also be due to factors such as demographic changes in an aging denomination, less of the denominational loyalty that used to keep people in the church of their upbringing, and a general North American trend toward less support for religious institutions in favor of a more fluid spirituality. One of the issues more specifically addressed below—that of women in ecclesiastical office—did result in a large exodus of members and churches and church splits in the 1990s, with many joining a new denomination started out of that conflict, the United Reformed Churches in North America. Some conversations are occurring in 2021 about similar potential changes that could result from decisions related to human sexuality, such as new or reconfigured denominations, as has been seen in other North American Christian churches, like the Presbyterian and Methodist denominations, and more recently, in the Reformed Church in America. It will likely take another five to ten years before that story can be told and understood.

Following are four church polity "case studies" that demonstrate this trend in the CRCNA of changing positions but allowing for variations in implementation.

Church Polity Case Study: Women in Ecclesiastical Office

The first case study, already mentioned above, is that of women in ecclesiastical office. While the story of the issue of women's ordination in the CRCNA goes back many years before 1995, a significant decision occurred in that year, just over twenty-five years ago. Prior to 1995, women had been ordained as deacons beginning in 1984, but only if their work was distinguished from that of elders.[6] And the offices of minister, elder, and evangelist (now renamed commissioned pastor) were not open to women. But in 1995, synod allowed women's ordination by exception in classes that believed all of the offices, including minister, should be open to women. Rather than making a change to the Church Order, classes

[6] *Acts of Synod 1984*, 655.

were allowed to take exception to the male requirement for ministers, elders and evangelists, based on their biblical convictions.[7] In the second half of the 1990s and the beginning of the first decade of the twenty-first century women were being ordained as elders, evangelists and ministers for the first time. The tension remained, though, between those who believed Scripture did not permit women to serve in these church offices and those who read Scripture differently. A study explaining both perspectives based on careful biblical interpretation was produced in 2000,[8] since synod recognized that both views could be drawn from Scripture, and in 2005 synod said that when a majority of the classes had taken the exception of 1995, synod would reconsider its position.[9] That occurred in 2006,[10] and in 2007 the male requirement was removed from the Church Order, while still allowing classes to take exceptions—now to not allow women office-bearers as delegates to their classis meetings.[11] Churches in those classes could ordain women but not delegate them to classis. Women did become delegates to synod after 2007, and in the ensuing years have served as officers of synod as well, including as clerks and vice presidents, but to date not yet as president. Today the tension still holds, though some in the four classes that continue to not allow women delegates wonder if their perspective is respected denominationally. But a proposal to celebrate the twenty-fifth anniversary of women's ordination in 2021 was changed to be a recognition, out of respect for those who cannot celebrate this event.[12]

So, this example demonstrates an issue by which synod allowed a change in our polity and criteria for office, but did not require churches to implement it, which had also been the case years before regarding women voting in congregational meetings. Synod had made a decision to allow women to vote already in 1957, the CRCNA's centennial year, but left it to

7 *Acts of Synod 1995*, 733-736.

8 *Acts of Synod 2000*, 351-407.

9 *Acts of Synod 2005*, 759-760.

10 *Acts of Synod 2006*, 721-724.

11 *Acts of Synod 2007*, 610-612.

12 *Minutes of the Special Meeting of the Council of Delegates in lieu of Synod 2020* [cancelled due to the Covid-19 pandemic], 456.

local churches to implement according to their own bylaws.[13] Some did so immediately, while others waited for decades before doing so. Today, however, all Christian Reformed churches allow women to vote.

Church Polity Case Study: Paedocommunion

Another significant issue in the CRCNA (and other North American denominations) has been paedocommunion, allowing children to partake of Holy Communion, or the Lord's Supper. Whereas the issue of women's ordination was dealt with in the CRCNA at the level of the Church Order, this matter involved confessional interpretations of Scripture related to the sacraments, not an allowance that different interpretations could be drawn from Scripture.

Historically, the CRCNA required profession of faith as the gateway to the table, but in the late 1980s and 1990s a movement toward young profession of faith began, driven by the desire to include children and young people at the table. In 1995 synod approved a procedure and liturgical form for the profession of faith of younger members and made changes to Church Order Article 59, allowing younger professing members to then take communion, but full membership responsibilities and privileges did not accompany that profession as in the past (commitment to the confessions, voting at congregational meetings, being eligible for office, and so on).[14] In the following decade, confusion resulted and the issue of children who had not professed their faith partaking of communion was still not solved.

In 2006, synod approved of opening the table to all baptized members in response to an overture,[15] but the church order changes proposed the next year to account for this decision were not approved in 2007 and synod instead appointed a faith formation committee to help the denomination understand the biblical theology behind this momentous change and discover ways to implement it thoughtfully.[16] That committee encouraged an early church

[13] *Acts of Synod 1957*, 90.
[14] *Acts of Synod 1995*, 712-721.
[15] *Acts of Synod 2006*, 730-731.
[16] *Acts of Synod 2007*, 653-657.

understanding of I Corinthians 11 as referring to the body of Christ as a community, and the need to welcome all and not prevent some from approaching the table, as some in Corinth had been doing, and as John Calvin seemed to do as well when he instituted the practice of profession of faith as a gateway to the table, similar to confirmation in the Roman Catholic Church. "Discerning the body" was seen as a communal activity, not just an individual one. In 2010 Synod adopted a guiding principle to allow all baptized members with age- and ability-appropriate faith to participate in the Lord's Supper in age- and ability-appropriate ways,[17] and the Church Order was changed to reflect this in 2011.[18] But the implementation was left to the elders in Church Order Article 59-a, which made room for various practices. Education about the change was needed for parents and children, and elders in different churches decided to either allow the parents to determine when their children were ready to take communion, hold a class and declare all children of a certain age welcome to the table, design a process for a child to meet with an elder who would note their age- and ability-appropriate faith and be welcomed individually to the table in worship, or to continue the traditional practice of requiring a profession of faith prior to partaking of communion. So, synod's decision allowed for change, but the local elders decided how to implement that change.

Case Study: Infant Baptism vs. Infant Dedication

In the past twenty-five years the CRCNA has also seen trends related to the sacrament of baptism, influenced by North American evangelicalism. Some newer members of church plants and even long-time members of established churches have been hesitant about infant baptism, preferring to wait for their children to grow up and choose baptism for themselves—also known as believer's baptism. As a result, infant dedication has become a practice or an option offered to parents in some churches, in spite of Synod 2011's clear instruction that ministers should refrain from doing infant

[17] *Acts of Synod 2010*, 810-812.
[18] *Acts of Synod 2011*, 829-830.

dedications in place of baptisms,[19] as infant dedication, in contrast to the teachings of the Reformed confessions, de-emphasizes baptism as a sign and seal of what God has done and overemphasizes, at the time of adult baptism, the role of human decision in salvation. A report to Synod 2012 from the Faith Formation Committee provided background and guidance on this matter, with helps for pastors and churches to address objections to the requirement of infant baptism.[20]

Interestingly, synod's decisions on this matter have been clear and do not allow for a variety of implementation responses. However, the decisions noted were based on the level of synod's decisions as interpretations of the confessions and of Reformed doctrine. And yet, churches themselves have used various practices and even ignored synod's decisions, with seeming impunity. Perhaps North American evangelicalism influences that encourage believer's baptism have had more influence in the past twenty-five years than the historic Reformed confessions of the CRCNA. They have been referred to as the "forms of unity" historically, but are they the glue that holds the CRCNA together today, or is another form of unity or influence of North American evangelicalism holding sway? The next case study may also demonstrate that influence more than the influence of historic Reformed doctrine as found in the confessions.

Church Polity Case Study: Human Sexuality

In the past twenty-five years there have been ongoing conversations about human sexuality, and especially about same-sex orientation and practice and same-sex marriage. The CRCNA's position on the subject was established in 1973 when synod gave pastoral advice to the churches and acknowledged that same-sex oriented persons might not be culpable for their condition, but also stated that same-sex behavior and practice was sinful and contrary to Scripture. This understanding has continued to form the core of the CRCNA's position on the topic.[21] Significantly, in the past twenty-five years as synod has addressed this issue twice

19 *Acts of Synod 2011*, 831-832.

20 *Acts of Synod 2012*, 425-433.

21 *Acts of Synod 1973*, 50-53.

more, in 2002 and 2016, it has continued to give pastoral advice to the churches.[22] So, unlike the church order level decisions on women's ordination and the confessional interpretation level issue of paedocommunion which led to church order changes, and the confessional interpretation in the disallowance of infant dedication in place of infant baptism, the matter of human sexuality has always been dealt with at the level of pastoral advice to the churches. It is not mentioned in the Church Order, except in a supplement regarding ministers solemnizing marriages.[23] And synod has never tied it to an interpretation of the confessions, including the Heidelberg Catechism's warnings about unchastity.[24]

Another study committee appointed by Synod 2016, called the "Committee to Articulate a Foundation-laying Biblical Theology of Human Sexuality," was set to report to Synod 2021, but has been deferred to 2022, since Synod 2021 was canceled due to the pandemic. The study committee had as part of its mandate to consider whether this issue should be recategorized as a confessional matter, even be considered a *status confessionis.*[25] After forty-seven years of categorizing synod's decisions on this issue as pastoral advice, that would be a major change and could lead people and churches to leave the CRCNA and cause some office-bearers to be unable to sign the Covenant of Office-bearers with integrity. In fact, the report of the study committee claims that the matter is already confessional, based on their interpretation of Scripture, but from a church polity and synodical history standpoint, that is not the case. Synod 2022 will have to decide whether to adopt the recommendations of the study committee, and change the nature of synodical decisions on this matter to that of confessional interpretation. Interestingly, the committee notes that even when matters are considered confessional interpretations and therefore required for office-bearers and confessing members, pastoral accommodations are allowed, such as when churches allow

22 *Agenda for Synod 2002,* 313-351; *Acts of Synod 2002,* 483-484

23 Supplement to Article 69-c, *Church Order.*

24 See DeMoor, Henry. *Christian Reformed Church Order Commentary,* 168-169.

25 *Acts of Synod 2016,* 915-916.

their members not to baptize their children.[26] This raises questions about what the impact of synod's decisions would be.

Further, one wonders whether Synod 2022 might allow for differences in implementation, or even differences in belief and biblical interpretation on the matter, as it has for women in office. Overtures to Synod 2021 in response to the most recent report indicate some churches and classes support the study committee's recommendations, but many others question them and argue for tolerance of different biblical interpretations.[27] Might it be possible that classes and churches could be allowed to vary in their perspective and practice while remaining united as a denomination, as was done with women in ecclesiastical office? Future synods will likely be wrestling with that question for many years.

Beyond these matters of synodical positions on various doctrinal and ethical issues, two other trends can be seen to support a more open perspective toward allowing for differences over the past twenty-five years: changes to our ecumenical charter and changed understandings of the offices of the church.

Changes in Approaches to Ecumenical Activities

Historically, the CRCNA, as a denomination founded in 1857 by immigrants from the Netherlands, tended to see ecumenical relationships as necessarily starting with those closest in belief and practice, originally out of a fearfulness of becoming too Americanized and losing cultural and theological distinctiveness. The immigrants that eventually established the CRCNA were at first part of the Reformed Church in America, one of the oldest Protestant churches in North America, but eventually separated from that denomination and established the CRCNA in 1857, in part to avoid the assimilation to American culture seen in the Reformed Church in America (RCA). Correspondence with other denominations was slow to start and for many years focused on those denominations closest to the CRCNA in

[26] https://www.crcna.org/sites/default/files/human_sexuality_report_2021.pdf, 145.

[27] *Agenda for Synod 2021*, 392-472.

doctrine and perspective, seemingly with an attitude of concern for being tainted by those who weren't as orthodox. Later the CRCNA was a leader in forming ecumenical organizations such as the Reformed Ecumenical Synod in 1946 and the North American Presbyterian and Reformed Churches (NAPARC) in 1975. But over time we realized that there were benefits to broader conversations and began to reach out to broader groups, even as some of these more focused groups, such as NAPARC, expelled us when we allowed women's ordination in 2002.

Our current ecumenical charter, adopted first in 1987 and revised in 2000 and 2006,[28] encourages unity and dialogue with other Christian churches, not just those theologically similar to us. The charter reminds us that we are united in Christ, and that "as there can be but one Lord, there can be but one church; one head, one body." It also notes that we are united with "the church of all generations and throughout the world," and that the unity of the church is "a gift and a task." We are united in Christ, and yet we must work at the task of being united as we work to overcome the scandal of division and disunity. Further, the charter recognizes that "unity is not uniformity," but "the manifold wisdom of God is to be made transparent through the church (Eph. 3:10). It is displayed not in the obliteration but in the reconciliation of diversity." The charter recognizes that healthy ecumenical relationships are not built on "monitoring and controlling behavior" that focuses on whether another denomination "had moved beyond the pale of theological and biblical integrity." Rather, healthy ecumenical relationships are "built on common interests and commitments to the ministry of the gospel and the mission to which that gospel calls the whole church."

The CRCNA Church Order is clear that the positions of other churches and ecumenical groups are not binding on the CRCNA unless our synod adopts them,[29] which makes room for broader conversations and influence in the ecumenical world. Today we are involved in the World

[28] https://www.crcna.org/eirc/ecumenical-relations/ecumenical-charter

[29] Article 50, *Church Order.*

Communion of Reformed Churches, the National Association of Evangelicals, and the Canadian Council of Churches, to name a few groups, and have for years participated in the Reformed-Catholic Dialogue. Further, in 2010 our synod adopted a mandate to engage in interfaith conversations as well.[30] This trend shows that as a denomination, the CRCNA is becoming more accustomed to and generous regarding conversations with those who hold different views.

At the same time that we are broadening our ecumenical approach, the CRCNA also has developed closer ties to its mother church, the RCA. Over the past decade more joint ministries have been developed at the denominational and classical levels, and a small but growing number of dual-affiliated and union churches exist that are members of both denominations. Further, on the synodical level, joint meetings of the synods of the CRCNA and the RCA occurred in 2014 and 2018. The Synod 2014 discussions, held in Pella, Iowa, resulted in a "Resolution on the Relationship between the RCA and the CRCNA: Past, Present and Future," which included a declaration "that the principle that guides us, and the intention that motivates us, is to 'act together in all matters except those in which deep differences of conviction compel [us] to act separately.'"[31] Known as the "Pella Accord," it has given momentum to joint ministries in recent years. But in 2021, as the RCA considers options for separation over the issue of human sexuality, one wonders if this also will be a matter for joint efforts, or if there are "deep differences of conviction" that will "compel us to act separately." Groups of CRC and RCA churches in western Canada and in the Midwest have talked about switching denominations over this issue, but with the CRCNA's synod delayed again to 2022, the outcome is uncertain.

Changes in Understanding and of Church Offices

A third trend in the polity of the CRCNA also allows for some variations on the local level, and that is development of the offices of commissioned pastor and deacon. While our

[30] https://www.crcna.org/eirc/interfaith-relations/interfaith-mandate
[31] *Acts of Synod 2014,* 503-504.

denomination began in 1857 with four offices—minister of the Word, professor of theology or doctor, elder, and deacon, the professor of theology eventually became a specialized minister of the Word, first noted in the revised 1965 Church Order. For several decades the CRCNA then included only three offices which were often aligned with the three-fold offices of Christ—prophet (minister), priest (deacon), and king (elder), but in 1978 synod added the office of evangelist as well.[32]

The groundwork for that new office had been developing for several decades. When small chapels and mission outposts were begun (today called new church developments, emerging churches, or church plants), leaders were needed to pastor these fledgling groups and facilitate their worship and ministry. Often begun by layworkers in evangelism and local indigenous leaders, these churches needed ministers to come in occasionally to administer sacraments and were not able to organize as incorporated churches while these unordained persons functioned as their leaders. Further, these groups were sometimes reluctant to organize, lest they would lose their beloved leaders because they would be required to form a council and call a minister of the Word as their pastor.

After many years of discussion, the church came to recognize that the understanding of the offices being aligned with the offices of Christ did not need to limit the number of offices, since all members actually are called to be prophets, priests and kings as they hold the office of the believer. So, synod finally declared evangelist to be the fourth office in 1978.[33] Synod expanded it to include a growing number of church staff positions in 2001,[34] rather than expanding the number of offices to accommodate youth pastors, worship directors, educational ministers, and so on. Realizing that the title "evangelist" was not always fitting for these positions, in 2004 the office was renamed "ministry associate,"[35] and in 2012 it was changed again to better describe those who held the office but were functioning as pastors, sometimes as

[32] De Moor, 22-23.

[33] *Acts of Synod 1978,* 77.

[34] *Acts of Synod 2001,* 506-508.

[35] *Acts of Synod 2004,* 548-549.

solo pastors. For them, "commissioned pastor" was a more accurate and honoring title for the office than "ministry associate."[36]

Today the office of commissioned pastor continues to develop, and the Church Order articles regarding it have not only gone through a series of changes in the past decade, but also a complete revision approved by Synod 2019. While in some ways the office of commissioned pastor has become more similar to the office of Minister of the Word, there remain some key differences, noted in Articles 23 and 24 of the Church Order and their Supplements, and in the Commissioned Pastor Handbook.[37] Those who are ordained as commissioned pastors are not required to have a seminary education, and can serve in emerging churches or alongside ministers in organized churches, and even serve as solo pastors of organized churches in particular circumstances where it is not practical or feasible to call a theologically-trained minister.[38]

The latest alteration to this office came in 2019 when synod decided to allow persons to be ordained as commissioned pastors and serve churches in that capacity while they are pursuing their theological education, as a bridge to ordination as a minister of the Word. This trend has made for more flexibility for persons called to ministry, even as seminary programs are now offered in online or hybrid formats, and candidates for ministry in the CRCNA are allowed to attend a wide variety of seminaries. In 2018, for the first time, more than half of the candidates approved for ministry had studied at other seminaries than the CRCNA's own Calvin Theological Seminary,[39] and in 2020 more than half of those candidates were women or non-white in ethnicity.[40] The approval of candidates in 2020 and 2021, interestingly, was done by the Council of Delegates, which functions as the interim committee of synod, because

36 *Acts of Synod 2012*, 741-742.

37 https://www.crcna.org/sites/default/files/Commissioned_Pastor_Handbook.pdf

38 Articles 23-24, *Church Order*.

39 https://www.thebanner.org/news/2019/06/crc-pastors-being-trained-in-other-seminaries

40 https://www.thebanner.org/features/2020/07/what-really-counts

synod itself did not meet due to the coronavirus pandemic. In the entire history of the CRCNA, through the Spanish flu and two World Wars, synod had never before been canceled. Perhaps one could say that in the last twenty-five years, that has been the most stunning change of all!

A second recent change related to the offices has been an increasing emphasis on and honoring of the office of deacon, often seen in the past as a steppingstone to becoming an elder in the church. A movement to revitalize the office of deacon resulted in several Church Order changes in 2015, to better honor the value of the parity of the offices, as established in Article 2 of the Church Order—that the offices "differ from each other only in mandate and task, not in dignity and honor."[41] Changes were made to nineteen different Church Order articles that year.[42] Largely due to a desire to value deacons and honor the parity of the offices, and the need to hear the voice and expertise of deacons in a greater scope of ministry, synod decided to require the delegation of deacons to classis and synod meetings, just like ministers and elders. This had the unintended effect of also increasing the number of women delegates to the broader assemblies, since there were more women serving in the office of deacon than in the other offices, even though churches were allowed but not required to ordain women to all the offices, as mentioned above.

Conclusion

All of these changes over the past twenty-five years—changes in doctrinal and ethical positions, in approaches to ecumenical relationships, and in the offices of the church—indicate a denomination that seeks to be true to its roots and the principles of its polity, while also adjusting to changing times and the need for greater flexibility as it continues to contextualize its mission and ministry in the North American context.

41 Article 2, *Church Order.*

42 *Acts of Synod 2015*, 656-669.

Church Polity: International Studies in Protestant Church Polity
Autumn 2021 2(1), pp. 17-36

The Ecclesiology of Vulnerability as a Starting Point for Building Friendly Relationship Between Church and State

Vera Loupatty

Church and state are two entities that are important for the realization of love, justice, and peace on this earth. Therefore, both are in a mutually supportive relationship to "fight" together for the sake of humanity. The history of the church showed that there were times church and state developed mutually beneficial relationships; however, at other times, both competed to be superior to one another. That the relationship that is not always mutually supportive, but also mutually beneficial as an entry point to strive for superiority over the other, occurs in the place where I live, the Minahasa region of North Celebes in Indonesia, and in my church, The Christian Evangelical Church in Minahasa (GMIM). For example, in mayors and governor elections, regional head candidates use the church as a "partner" to win certain candidates. For this

---

Vera Loupatty is on the Theology Faculty of the Christian University of Indonesia in Tomohon (UKIT). Corresponding Author email: veraloupatty2@gmail.com purpose, the church gets many benefits such as funds and facilities. In such a relationship, the church becomes a "political tool" of a particular candidate or political party. On the other hand, the church also uses the state to support both programs and personal/group achievements. In response to this reality, the church must weave a friendly relationship that based on an the ecclesiology of vulnerability. The vulnerability based on the vulnerability of God. His love is a vulnerable love because he is willing to embody with the sufferring of the world. In this relationship, the church and the state are equal companions who are willing to sacrifice for love, justice, and peace.

Introduction

I am interested in discussing the relationship between church and state because, in my view, church and state/government are often tempted to develop mutually beneficial or dominating relationships. In particular, I see this in the Minahasa region where I live and in my church, The Christian Evangelical Church in Minahasa (GMIM). The Minahasa region consists of seven regencies/cities. The ministry area of GMIM covers the entire Minahasa region and therefore is the biggest church in Minahasa. Because of this, the church becomes "a place" to gather mass power to achieve the political goals of the candidates for regional head elections. While the church does get many advantages and conveniences from this relationship, such that it looks to be a strong institution, but unfortunately, the church's prophetic voice becomes weak.

Based on this reality, vulnerability can be the spirit of the relationship between church and state. This vulnerability is rooted on the vulnerability of God. God was willing to become a human being in Jesus in order that He could embrace the suffering of the world. The Church is called to live into the vulnerability of God in her calling in this world. In order to be meaningful to others, the church must be willing to embrace the suffering of this world. This suffering is an encounter-space between God and human beings. On the foundation of the vulnerability, I envision the development of a friendly relationship between church and state. The relationship which based on an the ecclesiology of vulnerability makes the church and state as friends who struggle together to face and embrace the sufferings of the world. The design of this paper is as follows. First, I will discuss an ecclesiology of vulnerability, beginning by discussing a theology of vulnerability. Second, I will discuss the dynamics of the relationship between church and state in the church journey. Third, I will discuss a theology of friendship in order to build friendly relationship between church and state. Fourth, briefly, I will discuss the relationship between church and state in the 2016 GMIM Church Order. In that section, I will show the power in the church order to open opportunities for the church (GMIM) to build a meaningful relationship with the state.

Theology of Vulnerability

The term vulnerability comes from the Latin *vulnus* that means to wound and wounding.[1] Vulnerability is a universal fundamental part of the human body and life. According to Judith Butler, as cited by Joas Adiprasetya, vulnerability is an inherent dimension in human and social nature.[2] That is, a vulnerability refers to a human being whose body and mind are very easily sick and injured. Vulnerability makes people face lives full of risk, that which brings sickness, sadness, grief, and suffering. In Butler's view, vulnerability is an inherent dimension of human being. Vulnerability is not a mistake or something to be denied. It is not a the dark side of shame as a result of sin. It is a God's gift to everyone, therefore, as God's creation, everyone has their own uniqueness. According to Sturla J. Stalsett as quoted by Adiprasetya, "the inherent vulnerability of human beings encourages us to acknowledge and share vulnerable humanity while preventing the occurrence of a stigmatization of those who are socially considered more fragile."[3]

Thomas Reynolds discusses vulnerability that takes its point of departure from the vulnerable God. Reynolds

1 Kristine A. Culp, *Vulnerability and Glory: A Theological Account* (Louisville, Kentucky: Westminster John Knox Press, 2010), 3.

2 Joas Adiprasetya, *Gereja Paspandemi Merengkuh Kerapuhan* (Jakarat: BPK Gunung Mulia, 2021), 8.

3 Adiprasetya, *Gereja Pascapandemi*, 16.

acknowledges the transcendence of God, that God is the Almighty. Indeed, there is a distance between God the Creator and the creation. God is the eternal fellowship of the Father, the Son, and the Holy Spirit. God is in an inseparable relationship. The relationship between the Father, the Son, and the Holy Spirit penetrates each other as an affirmation of the strength of the relationship. Perichoresis describes the strength and eternity of fellowship based on love. The power of love makes God invite all of creation to dance together in divine dance. The love keeps the Father, the Son, and the Holy Spirit in fellowship and willingness to relate to human being and all creation. That love is implemented in Jesus Christ. "God is in solidarity with humanity at its most fundamental level, in weakness and brokenness."[4] "The power of God is absolute, but in order to relate to the world, He limits that power with absolute love."[5] The absolute love is not for the sake of achievement and self-glorification, but for embracing all of creation. God entered into the reality of human life in Jesus Christ who was born in Bethlehem and was crucified and died on Golgotha.

God's openness to relate to the world makes Him a vulnerable God. The willingness to relate to the world made God not keep His glory, "but emptied himself, taking the form of a slave, being born in human likeness" (Phil 2:7). God is The Almighty, but the willingness and openness to seek and embrace human beings makes Him a vulnerable God. From the highest place, He is willing to meet creation, becoming part of the reality of human life. Reynolds asserts "the transcendence of God is open to relationship."[6] God's openness to build a relationship is creative and participatory openness. He was willing to become a human in Jesus in order to be experienced as a traveling companion in this world. He expressed His involvement in human life and His willingness to suffer for human being. For creation, God is so foreign and distant, but about Him becomes real in Jesus. That God becomes flesh in Jesus is a commitment to presence with

4 Thomas E. Reynolds, *Vulnerable Communion, A Theology of Disability and Hospitality* (Grand Rapids, Michigan: Brazos Press, 2008), 197.

5 Reynolds, *Vulnerable Communion*, 156.

6 Reynolds, *Vulnerable Communion*, 156.

the sinful, the weak, and the helpless. He invites everyone to experience His love. His love is not a love that brings pleasure, but it is a risky love. "He was born on a cold night; He was known as a homeless preacher; He was sentenced to death."[7] Jesus lived a life full of risk but passed through every stage until He died on the cross. "Jesus Christ is the icon of a vulnerable God."[8] The vulnerability is a way for Him to reach out, embrace, and save humanity. Jesus taught that vulnerability is a part of life, therefore, vulnerability must be accepted and creatively managed in order for sustainable and meaningful life. The vulnerability had been inherent in Jesus since He came into the world. Truly, the vulnerable God is manifested in Jesus' suffering and God's grace is in the midst of tragedy.[9] God meets creation not as a mighty and invincible warlord, but as a vulnerable human. He gives hope not in the midst of luxury, but in the vulnerability. He accepts and dances with vulnerability in order to give hope and life to all creation.

As with Reynolds, Leonard Sweet emphasizes relationship writing about a binding relationship. "The incarnation is the new 'binding'—God 'binding' himself to humanity not in stone or ink but in flesh and blood. God doesn't offer final answers, the manacles of modernity, but binding relationships."[10] From the highest place, God came to the world to bind a relationship with the human being. In his writing, John Chrissavgis also talks about relationality. He admits that there is a distance between God and creation, so God is untouchable. There is a hierarchical relationship between God and creation. That distance, however, can be bridged by God's initiative. In this regard, Chrissavgis understands hierarchy between God and creation in a new perspective. God embodied in Jesus to become a part of reality of human life. The willingness to relate to creation is founded on a love that seeks, restores, heals, and saves. Thus, vulnerability is an inherent part of human beings

7 Reynolds, *Vulnerable Communion*, 200.
8 Reynolds, *Vulnerable Communion*, 197.
9 Reynolds, *Vulnerable Communion*, 166.
10 Leonard Sweet, *So Beautiful: Divine Design for Life the Church* (Colorado Springs, CO: David C. Cook, 2009), 116.

and a way for life to be meaningful to others.[11] Human beings can internalize vulnerability because of the Holy Spirit. According to Deborah van den Bosch as quoted by Adiprasetya, "The Holy Spirit enters into the vulnerability of creation and by grasping the vulnerable God offers divine help."[12] Furthermore, according to Adiprasetya, "embracing vulnerability by the Holy Spirit actually confirms the inseparable and intertwined two hands of God that are Son and Holy Spirit, in appreciating, caring for, and restoring a vulnerable and wounded life."[13] Jesus suffered and died on the cross, but He rose on the third day. Does His resurrection negate vulnerability? The risen Jesus met the disciples said, "Peace be with you. They were startled and terrified, and thought that they were seeing a ghost...Look at my hands and feet; see that it is I myself" (Lk 24:36-37, 38). When Jesus met them, Thomas, one of them was not with them, so he did not believe that his friends had seen Jesus. Jesus said to him, "Put your finger here and see my hands. Reach out your hand and put it in my side" (Jn 20:27).

The risen Jesus did not appear with authority as Lord of universe, but rather showed His scars. Thus, He carried the scars on the hands, feet, and stomach to show continuity before and after the resurrection. In addition, the scars also show His solidarity with those who are vulnerable. He brings vulnerability into His power and eternity. The Lord still carries scars on His body as a guarantee of hope that He embraces the sick and wounded.[14]

From all this, I conclude vulnerability as follows: (1) vulnerability is God's grace in everyone; (2) vulnerability is the "path" that must be taken in order for life to be meaningful to others; and (3) vulnerability becomes a space of encounter between God and all creation.

The church that binds itself to the Triune God is invited to experience God's vulnerable love. "The church is a mysterious extension of the Trinity into time, which not

11 John Chrissavgis, Obedience-Hierarchy and Ascetism the Concept of Spiritual Authority in the Church in *Atlas Serials*, t.t., 49-60

12 Adiprasetya, *Gereja Pascapandemi*, 26.

13 Adiprasetya, *Gereja Pascapandemi*, 26.

14 Sweet, *So Beautiful*, 200.

only prepares us for a life of unity, but allow us already to participate in it."[15] God calls the church that binds itself to Him to be a vulnerable communion. This means that vulnerable ecclesiology does not point to physical church, but rather to its commitment to embody the suffering of this world. God's love is to be real amidst all creation when the church opens arms and hearts to embody the sufferings of this world.

Friendly Relationship Between Church and the State

The Church and State are two distinct entities that should support each other for love, justice, and peace. In reality, church and state relations have ups and downs. Occasionally, church and state: (1) live in mutually supportive equality; and (2) compete against each other to be superior to the other.

In the early days of the church's development, Christians received quite unfair treatment from the Roman authorities. During the reign of Emperor Nero, Christians were accused of burning the city of Rome, so they were hunted and captured to be burned alive, torn apart by wild animal or crucified. In fact, some suspected that the city of Rome was burned down by Emperor Nero so that he could rebuild a larger and more luxurious palace.[16] During the reign of Emperor Domitian, Christians were accused of being rebels against the state. As emperor, he wanted to be worshipped as a god *(dominus et deus).* Worshipping the emperor as a god became a strictly enforced rule. Statues of the emperor were made and placed throughout the empire so that all citizens would worship him. Anyone who refused was accused of being a dissident and a rebel against the state. For Christians, the only God they would worship was the Triune God, so worshipping the emperor as a god was impossible. Thus, they never intended to oppose the emperor or become rebels against the state, but they were simply trying to express their faith. In reality, maintaining faith in Jesus Christ led to Christians

15 Steve Summers, *Friendship Exploring its Implications for the Church in Postmodernity* (New York: T&T Clark, 2009), 159.

16 Simon Sebag Montefiore, *Jerusalem the Biography* (Jakarta: PT Pustaka Alvabet, 2016), 148-149.

being persecuted by Rome. Imperial sanction was required for many things in the Roman empire, and because of the particular commitments of the Christians, this often led to poverty and becoming a marginal and voiceless people.

Until the reigns of Emperors Diocletian and Galerius, Christians were still subject to cruelty from the Roman authorities. "Christian officers were fired, Christian slaves could not become free men, church buildings were sealed, church property was confiscated, books and Bibles were burned."[17] This changed when Constantine became emperor of Rome, as he become a Christian. Since then, Christianity was not only no longer persecuted, but had even gained a special place in the Roman empire. Rather than Christianity being an impediment to one's progress and opportunity, the tables were turned and people began converting to Christianity in order to gain opportunities. Many people became Christians not because they loved Jesus, but in order to gain social and political privileges. In 313, the emperor issued Edict of Milan which gave formal and complete freedom to Christianity in the Roman empire. All church property had been confiscated by the state was returned.[18] In that freedom, the church grew into a powerful institution. The emperor saw Christianity to be very important for the unity and progress of the empire. If religion is strong then the state/empire becomes strong. In such an understanding, the church, as an institution, is very important. As ruler, Constantine gave everything to the church so that he managed her according to his will to achieve goals of the state. Christians were treated with special privileges such as gaining good positions in government and luxury facilities.[19]

Christianity became more important during the reign of Emperor Theodosius who made Christianity the state religion in 380. The blessing of the church became very important for the emperors in carrying out their duties for the progress of the country. Church leaders gained a special place in the

[17] H. Berkof, *Sejarah Gereja,* trans. I.H. Enklaar (Jakarta: Badan Penerbit Kristen Gunung Mulia, 1990), 48.

[18] Berkhof, *Sejarah,* 49.

[19] Diarmaid MacCulloh. *Groundwork of Christian History.* (London: Epworth Press, 1987), 89.

empire to obtain the pleasures and benefits derived from the state. The existence of paganism was rejected because it was against state regulations for Christianity was the state religion. The existence of Christianity changed significantly before and after 313—the Constantinian shift.[20] During the pre-Constantinian era, Christianity was persecuted, but after 313/the post-Constantinian era, Christianity persecuted. The unavoidable part of this situation was that the church was subject to emperor's orders.[21] The leader of church had the appearance of a bureaucrat or ruler with a higher position than the people and participation in the ministry was understood as an achievement rather than a gift of God. The church was subjected to the state which provided many advantages and luxuries, but the critical voice of the church was weakened. As a consequence of the power relationship between church and state, power, position, and enjoyment were important, and as a result, hierarchy in the church became central to perpetuate power and position.

In the course of history, church and state—pope and emperor—always try to dominate one over the other. Pope Leo I (450) argued that pope should govern the church and the world and as such he became a ruler of church and state.[22] King Charles the Great (768-814) succeeded in unifying Western Europe so that he managed to build a strong church-state. King Charles the Great was appointed as an emperor by the Pope so that his power was weakened.[23] In 860, Pope Nikolaus made Rome the throne of Peter and the center of the empire so that he could govern both church and state. During the reign of emperor Otto in Germany, he replaced princes who disagreed with him with bishops so that bishops governed church and government. Bishops were elected and appointed by the emperor for the sake of achieving political interests.[24]

20 James A. Reimer, Trinitarian Orthodoxy, Constantianism, and Theology from A Radical Protestant Perspective. In *Faith to Creed: Ecumenical Perspectives and the Affirmation of the Apostle Faith in the Fourth Century*, Ed. Mark Heim (Grand Rapids, MI: William B. Eerdmans Publishing Company, 1991), 131.

21 Berkhof, *Sejarah*, 50-51

22 Berkhof, *Sejarah*, 73.

23 Berkhof, *Sejarah*, 74.

24 Berkhof, *Sejarah*, 80.

This reality perpetuates the practice of simony—buying and selling positions in the church. Kings and nobles competed for positions in the church as a way to arrange church and state in order to easily gain advantages. The Emperor had power to give the office of bishop to the highest bidder. The same thing was done by a bishop to someone who wanted a position in the church. Moral decadence among church leaders was protested through the renewals of Cluny (910) which sought to return the church to its true function. Some key points of Cluny's renewal: "1. Monasteries must be ruled directly by pope; 2. King and nobility may no longer allowed to interfere in the affairs of churches and monasteries; 3. Monks must obey, discipline and live more righteously."[25] Pope Gregory VII sought to limit the emperor's authority in terms of choosing popes. For him, the emperor had no right to choose the pope, because there was a great conflict between the pope and the emperor. He asserted that world power could only be granted by the pope, therefore the pope appointed the emperor. The struggle of Pope Gregory was reinforced in the Worms agreement of 1122. Nevertheless, the emperor was still given the right to give the title of king to whomever he wanted. The emperor still had an authority to regulate ecclesiastical affairs, even though that authority has been severely restricted. Pope Innocent III (1198-1216) argued that the pope was less great than God, but greater than a human being, so that he is not only Peter's vicar, but even the vicar of Christ. He had the power to govern church and state, and therefore all the kings are subject to him. The pope's great power led to the continuation of simony among church leaders for power, office, and wealth.[26] The desire to rule over both church and state was also seen in Pope Boniface VII (1294-1303) who issued the Bull Unam Sanctam (1320) which ascribes to the pope two swords, namely spiritual and worldly power.

The impact of this power relationship between church and state, as in the reign of Emperor Constantine, the prophetic voice of church was weakened. The church leaders positioned themselves as government officials to get many

[25] Berkhof, *Sejarah*, 80.

[26] Berkhof, *Sejarah*, 87.

advantages from the state. Ultimately, church focuses more on achieving various forms of pleasure and luxury than the ministry of love and justice.

Power and position, enjoyment and luxury resulted in increasingly visible moral decadence among church leaders in the late Medieval period. Pope Innocent III had a number of illegitimate children. Pope Alexander VI (1492-1503) liked to collect gold and women.[27] The clergy in Rome were known for their hedonism and were involved in sex scandals, drunkenness, and parties. Pope Leo X, patron of the artists, was not interested in spiritual issues.[28] Furthermore, Eddy Kristiyanto explained, moral decadence was not only occurred in Rome, but also in Germany, and was even worse. Bishops made wealth a purpose in life and neglected ministry. Life in monasteries became corrupted when the lifestyle of nobility influenced it. The government gave church officials special privilege in terms of taxation being granted a number of dispensations, whereas the poor were forced to pay taxes to the government. In Germany, the government gave privileges to the clergy by making them landlords. They enjoyed a life of wealth and luxury, and as landlords, they oppressed the peasants.[29]

Church and State Relations in the Reformation

This brings us, then, to the church and state relations according to Martin Luther, Ulrich Zwingli, and John Calvin. Their are varied enough to see development of understanding. I will, however, discuss more about Calvin's views, as the church order which I will discuss is in a Calvinist tradition.

Martin Luther distinguished between church and state very clearly. For him, the church is concerned with spiritual government and the state is concerned with secular government—two kingdoms. The church performs its duties according to God's will in guidance of Holy Spirit. Meanwhile, the government carries out its duties with the "sword of power" to enforce civil law. This was done by the

[27] Eddy Kristiyanto, *Reformasi dari Dalam Sejarah Gereja Zaman Modern* (Yogyakarta: Kanisius, 2004), 44.

[28] Kristiyanto, *Reformasi*, 45.

[29] Kristiyanto, 35.

government not to perpetuate violence, but rather to restrain sin. For Luther, government–in this case kings, princes, and judges—were chosen by God to carry out God's work in social life. The church and the state each and together carried out God's will.[30] Even according to Luther, existence of civil law was God's way of controlling people from sin. He asserted, "God ruled the world including the church, through princes, and judges. The church was in the world and thus subjected itself to the rules of the world."[31] On the one hand, Luther distinguished between the governments of church and state, but on the other hand, he even positioned the state above the church, for when the church leaders were trying to execute him to eliminate the challenge to papal authority, he survived because the German princes protected him.

Ulrich Zwingli developed church and state relations much like Luther, but he found it difficult to see the church and state as two entities. According to him, "the life of the state is no different from the life of the church. Church leaders and rulers obeyed God because they were entrusted to uphold God's rule over the city (Zurich)."[32]

Furthermore, John Calvin argued that church and state are tools that God uses to reveal His will to the world. Both were two distinct entities that were not superior to each other.[33] The Church and the state were two equal entities; support each other, but not depend on each other. Like Luther and Zwingli, Calvin also argued the church and state both accepted duty from God, but he firmly distinguished duties for church and state and did not confuse the two tasks. Calvin did not see a conflict between church and state, for both received duties from God. "God was sovereign over both church and state, for both are spiritual entities."[34] He asserted, "the political power of a calling, which is not only holy and lawful before God, but also the holiest and most

[30] Allister E. McGrath, *Sejarah Pemikiran Reformasi,* Trans. Liem Sien Kie (Jakarta: Badan Penerbit Kristen Gunung Mulia, 1997), 270.

[31] In McGrath, *Sejarah Pemikiran*, 272.

[32] In McGrath, *Sejarah Pemikiran,* 276.

[33] A.A. Yewangoe, *Hidup dari Pengharapan* (Jakarta: Badan Penerbit Kristen Gunung Mulia, 2017), 185.

[34] Yewangoe, *Hidup,* 228.

honorable of all callings in all mortal environments."[35] He viewed, perhaps aspirationally, the role of the state to create a conducive atmosphere for all to live, including the church. For him, "the state is a tool for communion with God."[36] For Calvin, an important theological basis for this high respect for the relationship between church and state was that the responsibility for helping to restore the image of God in human beings was not for the church alone but also for the state.[37] The Church remained a church, because she could not be a state. Likewise, the state remained a state, because it could not be a church. The church (religion) and the state (social order) came together in life. Both had different ways of carrying out their duties and responsibilities, but both carried out God's will and strived for God's will to be realized in daily life of the people. Calvin referred to the government as representatives of God for which the church and all citizens should pray so that they could carry out their duties and responsibilities properly.

Citizens should support the government in enforcing justice and truth. If the government became tyrannical, then the church should declare it unsupportable. He referred to "tyranny as the devil."[38] However, he did not think that the people should criticize the government by way of rebellion. He believed that God called certain people to urge and suppress the government, and therefore the people should not rebel against the government. Therefore, he strongly disagreed with the anarchist actions of the Anabaptists who wanted go so far as to abolish civil rule. For him, the thought was very inhumane and even against God's will, because the government, as an institution, came from God.[39]

In his thinking, Calvin tried to put forward the understanding that because both church and state came from God, theocracy was inevitable in the life of the state. This,

[35] John Calvin, *Institutio,* trans. Ny. Winarsih and J.S. Aritonang (Jakarta: Badan Penerbit Kristen Gunung Mulia, 2000), 315.

[36] Yewangoe, *Hidup,* 228.

[37] W. Balke "Pandangan Calvin Mengenai Gereja dan Negara." In *Ecclesia Reformata Semper Reformanda,* eds. M.L. Batlajery and Th. Van den End. (Jakarta: Badan Penerbit Kristen Gunung Mulia, 2014), 165.

[38] Yewangoe, *Hidup,* 231.

[39] Calvin, *Institutio,* 314.

of course, was motivated by the superiority of Christianity in the late Medieval period. This atmosphere was certainly existent in the city of Geneva where Calvin worked as well. He denounced the superiority of the church over the state, as well as the superiority of the state over the church, therefore he sought to develop an equal relationship between church and state. The relationship is based on the desire of God for people to live out God's will on earth. Observing Calvin's understanding, there were times when the church could be superior to the state because of the growing understanding of theocracy; and there were times when the state could be superior to the church because Christianity that dominated the state. For example, in the matter of applying church discipline, Calvin fought so that it became the authority of the church, not the state. This made Calvin's efforts to realize an independent church and an equal relationship between church and state difficult. Nevertheless, I appreciate Calvin's efforts in his day toward realizing the reality that church and state are in an equal relationship that both strive to carry out God's will which brings prosperity and good to all creation.

Calvin emphasized the obedience of the citizen to the government. A citizen may express disagreement with the government, but are not allowed to rebel. This understanding, however, weakens the critical voice of the church. Beginning from the foundation that the civil government comes from God, the church not only prays, but also speaks up and acts if the government becomes unjust in carrying out its duties. As I have stated, the Christianity that became the "soul" of the state made Calvin appreciate the government officials who were also church officials. Thus, in my opinion, church and state relations should be understood in the context in which he lived and worked. I agree with Calvin's understanding that church and state are two equal entities that come from God to create prosperity and goodness for all creation. However, ideas that the church can be superior to the state, and *vice versa*–the state can be superior to the church–should give way to a friendly relationship between church and state. I will discuss this in the next section of this article, where I discuss the friendly relationship between church and state, and argue that vulnerability becomes starting point of such relationship.

The Friendly Relationship Between the Church and the State

Everyone who lives in this world must have a friend, because no one can live alone. As social beings, everyone needs other people. In fact, Jesus also greeted the disciples with friends.

> This is my commandment, that you love one another as I have loved you. No one has greater love than this, to lay down one's life for one's friends. You are my friends if you do what I command you. I do not call you servants any longer, because the servant does not know what the master is doing; but I have called you friends, because I have made known to you everything that I have heard from my Father (Jn 15:12-15).

Jesus greeted the disciples as friends. He no longer called them servants, but friends. In Jesus' day, the use of the word servant could have negative connotations. The word servant was associated with slavery and meant that a servant did not have many rights. A servant had no right to question their master, for they must always agree to the will of the master. A master-servant relationship creates hierarchy, domination, and power to able to continue and disrupt relationships between humans. In this relationship, the master is the subject and the servant is the object. Master and servant are thus in an unequal relationship. Jesus wanted a friendly relationship between Him and the disciples. The relationship was based on love. Why did Jesus want a friendly relationship between them? In Jesus' context, friendship was familiar. If two people have promised to be friends, then the promise was done by oath. Thus, the promise binds both for life.

When Jesus greeted the disciples as friends, He greatly appreciated them. Friendship caused them to build a heart-to-heart relationships so that they were closer and more open. They knew each other as precious and loving persons. They were not in a dominating relationship, but in a mutually empowering relationship. The friendly relationship that

Jesus meant was not just a habit that applied in the context of their lives. He said that there was no greater love than the love than to lay down one's life for one's friends (Jn 15:13). As a friend, Jesus loved His friends and gave His life to them.

According to Eduard Zaragoza, Jesus' sacrifice is rooted in trinitarian relations. God seeks creation and makes friends with them and then sacrifices for them. The relationship with the Triune God makes Christians as persons who open up to being part of the communal life process, both in church and society. Christians who are aware that they are part of others will produce an open fellowship to this world. It means that no believer or fellowship/church can live isolated from each other and this world.[40]

Jesus' call to His disciples is also His call to the church. The calling arises from vulnerable love. As explained at the beginning of this article, vulnerability is rooted in fellowship of the Father, the Son, and the Holy Spirit. The Church is called to live in God's vulnerable and risky love that is not oriented toward pleasure and luxury, but is oriented toward a willingness to take part in the sufferings of this world. The vulnerability becomes a space of encounter with God and fellow human beings.

The church and the state are two distinct entities with their respective duties. Both are friends who are willing to walk and fight together for the good of creation. In the friendly relationship, effort is not spent seeking superiority over the other. Friends do not live in relationships that dominates each other but they are willing to build a heart-to-heart relationship in which each side feels fully accepted.[41] The Church internalizes a vulnerable and risky life. It does not pursue of luxury, pleasure, and profit, but it is love that embodies in the sufferings of the world. A love is ready to embrace the vulnerable and wounded world. Based on this love, the church will not take advantage of the state. The state will also not use the church to maintain the status quo. The friendly relationship based on vulnerability is an

[40] Edward C. Zaragoza, *No Longer Servants, but Friends* (Nashville: Abingdon Press, 1999), 69.

[41] Brian Edgar, *God is Friendship* (Wilmore, KY: Seedbed Publishing, 2013), 24.

invitation for the state to become traveling companions with the church, both of which are willing to be broken to create love and justice for all people. Thus, the relationship between church and state is not only equal, but also ready to live with the suffering of the world.

The Relationship of Church and State in the 2016 GMIM Church Order

The Minahasanese knew the gospel of Jesus Christ from evangelists who came from faraway countries and institutions. Portuguese, Spanish, Dutch East India Company (VOC), and Netherlands Missionary Society (NZG) evangelists played a role in evangelizing in Minahasa land. After the VOC disbanded, the Dutch government took the power, including ecclesiastical life. King Willem I, who failed to unite Protestant churches in the Netherland, had the opportunity to realize this purpose in Indonesia. In 1815, the government determined that the operationalization of Protestant churches in Indonesia would be carried out by the state, in this case the Ministry of Commerce and Colonization. The Dutch government, then, governed Protestant churches in Indonesia.[42]

The state governed the church as it governed the civic life. Church ministers were treated as state employees, therefore the state was responsible for their living expenses. In regulations of the Protestant Church in Indonesia (1938), Article 2, regarding the Church Assembly, "church officials consist of: pastor, elder, and deacon." In such an arrangement, hierarchical relations between church and state are inevitable. Pastor, elder, and deacon were subject to the Dutch government because they were government employees. The relationship between them was also a hierarchical relationship, one being higher than the other. This all shows that hierarchy in the church (GMIM) has strong historical roots, and the hierarchy is still visible in the 2016 GMIM Church Order.

[42] G.P.H. Locher, *Tata Gereja Gereja Protestan di Indonesia, Suatu Sumbangan Pikiran Mengenai Sejarah dan Asas-asasnya* (Jakarta: Badan Penerbit Kristen Gunung Mulia, 1997), 45.

In the 2016 GMIM Church Order, church and state relations are stated in the Preamble section:

> The Evangelical Christian Church in Minahasa is called to ally, testify and serve in the land of Minahasa, in the Unitary State of the Republic of Indonesia based on Pancasila and the Constitution of the Republic of Indonesia in 1945, even around the world, as an expression of heart, soul, mind, and strength. GMIM as an independent Part Church and Protestant Church in Indonesia since September 30, 1934, based on: Staatsblaad Dutch East Indies number 563/1934, dated September 17, 1934 and Decree of the Director General of Guidance of Protestant Christian Community Department of the Republic of Indonesia, number 91/1992, dated October 5, 1992 (TG GMIM, 2016).

GMIM recognizes that the land of Minahasa, the state of Indonesia, and the world are places for fellowship, witness, and service. GMIM is a church that is grounded in the earth, where it lives and works. This is further emphasized by the existence of several letters from the state as evidence that GMIM is an institution that follows formal provisions in Indonesia. The formulation of church and state is limited to these things. The church order does not formulate in more detail how the relationship is built and maintained. According to Lazarus Purwanto, the church order is a place where the church can reveal her identity. Identity is related to many things, including how the church builds relation with the state. The detailed relationship between church and state in the preamble of the church order is a good thing to guide the church in formulating the rules in the church order.[43]

The hierarchical legacy of the Dutch government should be a warning for GMIM so that the church order does not become a comfortable place for hierarchy to continue to live and develop. In the past, hierarchical relations between church and state were strong as a consequence of the state governing the church. Realizing this, GMIM should develop a

[43] Lazarus Purwanto, "Church Order and Church Identity Challenges and Opportunities for Churches in Indonesia to Express Their Identity Through Church Order," *Church Polity*, 1, no. 1 (2020): 21.

friendly relationship with the state, but this has not received as much attention as expected. I think this has an impact the hierarchy continuing to have a place in the life of the church, more specifically in the church order. In the Basic Order, Chapter IV, Article 17: "The Synod Assembly is the highest decision maker." The word highest refers to something higher and lower. Practically, the word is common in government, but not in the church. Hierarchy is a historical heritage that finds a safe and comfortable place in the church order.

Based on the Basic Order, Chapter III, Article 8, "The Evangelical Christian Church in Minahasa as an independent church is organized in the Synodal Presbyterian system based on the government of the Lord God in Jesus Christ."

> The presbyterian-synodal system knows neither the higher nor the highest. The system is known for its wider courts and is attended by representatives of local churches. So, matters that have not been discussed/decided at the congregational level will be discussed at the region/synod. Historically, in the XVI century this appeared in the spirit of anti-independentism. Although the autonomy of the local church is emphasized, the danger of absolute independentism must also be avoided. Through the interchurch relationship manifested in the trial, the church will be able to relate in one common confession of faith to a joint ministry.[44]

The use of the word highest has implications for the relationship between church officials; some are higher and some are lower, whereas presbyterian-synodal system promotes collective-collegial leadership.

> The collective nature puts pressure on the unity of the assembly institutions. In general, collectivity means all pastors, deacons, and elders think and act to serve in one unity and in togetherness. In this regard, none of them can be ahead and dominant against the other. Organizational positions and functions (e.g., chairman, secretary, and treasurer) are defined primar-

[44] Lazarus Purwanto, "Spiritualitas Sistem Presbiterial-Sinodal dalam Penataan/Hukum Gereja," Seminar, 2016, 4.

> ily for the sake of organizational sustainability and do not contain any primacy and dominance at all. Here comes the *primus inter pares* principle, "the first (not the foremost!) among those who are equal or equal."[45]

GMIM's selection of presbyterian-synodal system should also be a reminder that hierarchy has no place in the church order. But instead, hierarchy appears explicitly in the church order with using the term "the highest." Therefore the church order provides a wide space for the hierarchy to grow up in the church. This is an indication that the church leaders and the church members have become accustomed to hierarchy, power, and position. In my view, hierarchy, power, and position are strengthened in the church so that the church adopts the bureaucratization of state government into the ministry of the church.

It is possible for the friendly relationship between church and state to be developed by GMIM. In such relationship, church and state can respect each other's identities and commit to embrace the vulnerability of the world and embody with the suffering of the world. In fact, GMIM is open to evaluating the power relation contained in the church order. Thus, the church order really functions to serve the church in carrying out God's will in this world.

Conclusion

The friendly relationship between church and state which is based on the ecclesiology of vulnerabulity should be an alternative ecclesiology to be developed by churches, including GMIM. In this relationship, the church and the state will not build a relationship that is oriented toward profit, power, and enjoyment, but is oriented toward the willingness to sacrifice for the sake of the life of the entire creation. This understanding is urgently needed by the vulnerable world because of disease/virus (COVID-19), natural disasters, poverty, etc. The willingness of the church and the state to embrace the vulnerable world raises the hope that the world is household for all creation to experience love, justice, and peace.

45 Purwanto, "Spiritualitas," 4.

Church Polity: International Studies in Protestant Church Polity
Autumn 2021 2(1), pp.37-66

Agencies of the Gospel: Mission Challenge and Opportunities in the Australian Lutheran Church

Mark Vainikka
Luke van der Laan

This article explores challenges and opportunities faced by the LCA in relation to its church order and the governance of its agencies. LCA agencies are agencies of the gospel in their communities. This is a considerable strength of LCA agencies and institutional leaders. The LCA operates significant aged-care, community service and educational agencies that receive state and federal government funding. The LCA, however, finds itself in an increasingly complex regulatory operating environment. This is especially problematic due to an elevated level of competition from other not-for-profit and for-profit

---

Mark Vainikka is Bishop of the Lutheran Church of Australia, Queensland District. Corresponding Author email: mark.vainikka@lca.org.au

Luke van der Laan is Associate Professor and Programme Director, University of Southern Queensland ORCID ID: 0000-0003-2275-8974.

agencies and coincides with substantial shifts in the Christian church's place in Australia's national narrative. Church attendance and membership continue to decline. However, the size and number of many of LCA's agencies continue to grow. This has resulted in a church that is decreasing in membership and worship attendance yet has agencies that are increasing in size, governance, and management complexity. The LCA's shrinking congregational base and growing agency base presents the LCA with fundamental questions relevant to its future. Is the LCA primarily a gathering of congregations with agencies to aid and further the church's missional work? Or, is the LCA primarily an entity with growing agencies with a reducing number of congregations supporting the work of church agencies? The Lutheran church's ecclesiology strongly indicates the former, while a rapidly changing place in the Australian public space puts pressure on the church to conform to the latter. This paper presents the outcomes of a study seeking to differentiate these perspectives and consider its implications on the governance of the LCA and church bodies more broadly.

The LCA is part of the global Lutheran tradition, with over seventy million Lutherans worldwide. While the LCA is small compared to many other Lutheran churches globally, its educational and community care institutions place it in contact with tens of thousands of Australians weekly.

Australia has a long history of church agencies providing welfare and educational services on the governments' behalf.[1] The Christian church's place in the Australian public space has also been helped by the church functioning as a provider of government-funded welfare and educational services. However, it has also generated public condemnation, as highlighted by the Royal Commission into Institutional Responses to Child Sexual Abuse established in 2013. This represents a tension between the 'halo effect,' or goodwill to society created by church agencies and its legitimacy in the

[1] John Murphy, "Church and state in the history of Australian welfare," in *Church and state in old and new worlds*, ed. Hilary M Carey and John Gascoigne, Brill's series in church history (Leiden, Netherlands: Brill, 2011).

view of the public, government and critically, its membership and mission.

As church attendance and membership continue to decline in Australia, church institutions and agencies are often the filter by which the church is evaluated in society. For the Christian church, social inclusion can be helped by the presence of its institutions and agencies in society, but it can also be challenged due to the misgivings and failures of the same institutions and agencies.[2] Therefore, the Christian church in Australia is not only a theological construct or an ecclesiastical entity, but an organization in society with corporate and community responsibilities.

The LCA has evolved from an entity that solely connects with society by gathering for worship, into an organization that also engages with society through its agencies such as community services, education and aged-care. The impact and contributions of these activities compound into what is known as the 'Halo Effect,' a significant socioeconomic contribution to communities.[3]

How the church is perceived in Australian society is also changing, not only through a growing disengagement with organized religion, but also through the new ways the church engages with society. Hence, for many people, their primary contact with the LCA and other Australian mainline churches is no longer through Sunday morning worship or pastoral acts such as the sacrament of baptism, but through their children's schooling or their elderly parents' nursing care.

As these contact points are also commercial, the church in Australia across denominations needs to consider how it should govern itself within this changed societal and governmental context. Further, greater understanding is needed on how to fulfill their ecclesiastical mission by doing this faithfully in terms of its statements of confessions and

2 Andrew P Lynch, "Negotiating social inclusion: The Catholic Church in Australia and the public sphere," *Social Inclusion* 4, no. 2 (2016), https://doi.org/10.17645/si.v4i2.500.

3 Mike Wood Daly, "Taxing faith: Halo effect and the implications of taxing Canadian places of worship," *Studies in Religion/Sciences Religieuses* (14 October 2020), https://doi.org/10.1177/0008429820957643.

self-understanding, and in relation to other churches, external regulations, and the expectations of society at large. This paper presents an LCA perspective of these contemporary challenges in order to promote a holistic understanding of the role and functioning of the church with the aim of remaining relevant in its contributions to society according to its mission.

The Church as an Organization in Society

In an increasingly secular society such as Australia, the church has had to accept that often society perceives the church like any other organization. The church is expected to be a good corporate citizen of Australia and fulfill the same, if not higher, expectations and demands placed on other organizations by law. Further to this, as the church occupies its spot in the marketplace through its institutions, it is met with commercial expectations and norms of how one must act as a commercial entity, albeit a not-for-profit one. Such expectations and norms can create pressure, especially for church agencies, to expand, compete, and respond to market forces.

However, the church's visibility is not based on its organizational visibility but the presence of the marks of the church, namely the Word and the sacraments. The church cannot fault society for seeing it as simply another organization among other organizations, but neither can it be seduced by its place in society on the basis of its organizational visibility. If the church did this, it would be abdicating as a church, "Forgetting the crucial element which alone can make its visible aspects into a true church: the Spirit, which invisibly controls the visible church, making it spiritually alive, fruitful and credible."[4]

The LCA's development from a small ethnically German immigrant church in the 1830s in the state of South Australia to a national provider of educational, aged-care and community care services, presents several governance and church polity related challenges and questions. Many church-run institutions in Australia grew from small

[4] Hans Küng, *The church*, Tenth Impression (1992) ed. (Kent: Burns & Oates, 1968), p. 37.

and humble beginnings. As regulatory requirements on government-funded church-run institutions continue to expand, the church's need to exercise best practice in all areas of its operations has become more acute.

There are also non-regulatory reasons why the church should focus on growing governance capability. Bad leadership, inadequate management skills and incompetent governance may result in people being harmed. As an entity based on the public good, the church by definition should do its utmost not to harm. Therefore, the church, possibly more than most other organizations, has a moral and ethical responsibility to develop and implement best practice in all areas of its organization and take seriously its call to protect people from harm.

Ordering of the Church in the Lutheran Tradition

As an organization in modern-day Australia, the LCA is not only defined as a gathering of people where God's Word is preached and the sacraments administered according to the gospel. Since the LCA exists as a visible gathering of people organized legally in Australia according to the laws of the Commonwealth of Australia, it is also a legal entity, defined as an organization like other similar organizations. LCA's constitutions and by-laws interpret the church's theology and ecclesiology for its current geographical context and time. They guide how the LCA interacts and functions parochially and with and within society.

The LCA's basic governance structure can be defined by the Wilhelm Maurer coined term 'synodical-episcopate,' where the principles of the structure also apply to the pastor at the congregational level.[5] In the LCA's context, the term 'synodical-episcopate' highlights the relationship between the office of the holy ministry and the community of the faithful gathered together. The word 'synodical' in this context acknowledges that congregations and parishes have voluntarily agreed to join together to work toward fulfilling the mission of the Christian church in the world. The word 'episcopate' in this context is used in the sense it is found

[5] Michael Root, "Church law and governance in the Lutheran tradition," *Jurist* 60 (2000).

in the Lutheran confessions, of a person who serves as one looking after people's spiritual needs through sacramental ministry.[6]

In this synodical-episcopate dynamic, "The power of bishops is that command given by Christ to proclaim the Gospel, to use the ministry of the keys to forgive or retain sins, and to administer the sacraments."[7] On the other hand, the congregation is called to judge the exercise of the office of bishop and pastor and if the bishops teach contrary to the Word, the people should not obey.[8] This juxtaposition of the office of the holy ministry and the community of the people of God provides the essential structure of Lutheran church polity.

Lutheran ecclesiology identifies the congregation as the church's foundational entity and the locus of sacramental ministry, where the church's missional work is primarily located.[9] This foundational understanding of Lutheran ecclesiology means that all other structures are an extension of the congregation, whether church agencies, regional or national offices. From the perspective of Lutheran ecclesiology, the congregation is at the center of church life in a synodical Lutheran church. This is an important consideration in the light of the LCA's growing institutions.

The German text of the Lutheran church's Augsburg Confession Article VII defines the church as a gathering of people:

> It is also taught that at all times there must be and remain one holy, catholic church. It is the assembly of all believers among whom the gospel is purely preached and the holy sacraments are administered according to the gospel.[10]

6 Kurt E Marquart, *The church and her fellowship, ministry, and governance*, ed. Robert D Preus, 13 vols., vol. IX, Confessional Lutheran dogmatics, (St Louis, Mo.: The Luther Academy, 1990).

7 AC XXVIII Robert Kolb and Timothy J Wengert, "The Book of Concord: The confessions of the Evangelical Lutheran Church," ed. Robert Kolb and Timothy J Wengert (Minneapolis, MN.: Fortress Press, 2000), 96.

8 XXVIII Kolb and Wengert, "The Book of Concord: The confessions of the Evangelical Lutheran Church."

9 AC VII Kolb and Wengert, "The Book of Concord: The confessions of the Evangelical Lutheran Church."

10 Kolb and Wengert, "The Book of Concord: The confessions of the Evangelical Lutheran Church," 42.

Hence, in Lutheran ecclesiology, the church does not exist without the preaching of the gospel in accordance with Scripture and the administration of the sacraments according to the gospel. As Luther argued, "Where the word [gospel] is, there is faith; and where faith is, there is the true church."[11]

For Luther, the external preaching of the Word and the visible administration of the sacraments were essential also from a pastoral perspective. For Luther, the foundation of pastoral care was the forgiveness of sins through the means of grace. It was through these external means, Luther argued, that all Christians could be sure of their forgiveness. In his 1535 commentary on Genesis, Luther wrote:

> Word, Baptism, and the Eucharist are our light bearers today...We can state with certainty that where the Eucharist, Baptism, and the Word are, there are Christ, forgiveness of sins, and eternal life...Therefore this gift is something inexpressible: that God not only deigns to speak to men through the Word but adds to the Word visible signs of grace, such as Baptism, the Eucharist, and absolution.[12]

Therefore, for Luther, God deals with humankind on two levels, in a visible and a non-visible way, both inwardly and outwardly. God deals with humankind outwardly through the means of grace and inwardly through the Holy Spirit, faith, and other gifts. However, for Luther and the Lutheran confessions, the church was not identified by individual members, but by the marks attached to the church, namely the Word and the sacraments, preached and administered according to the gospel.[13]

The LCA's Incarnational Mission

While not dissimilar to many other organizations in society from a legal and organizational perspective, the church's identity makes the church a complex entity to define

11 Martin Luther, *Church and ministry I*, 55 vols., vol. 39, ed. Eric W Gritsch, Luther's Works, (Minneapolis, MN: Fortress Press, 1970), XII.

12 Martin Luther, *Lectures on Genesis: Chapters 1-5*, 55 vols., vol. 1, ed. Jaroslav Jan Pelikan, Luther's Works, (Saint Louis, MO: Concordia Publishing House, 1.5.1958, 1958), 249-50.

13 Marquart, *The church and her fellowship, ministry, and governance*, IX.

in organizational terms. This presents the church with a unique dilemma; how to reconcile its understanding and self-identity with its contemporary corporate role in society.

Purely from an organizational perspective, the LCA embodies a problematic mission to define, and its goals are also difficult to quantify. A church's mission is not the same as that of corporations: profit maximization. Neither is it the same as that of many not-for-profits, for example, solely the education of the young, the support of the aging, or the sheltering of the homeless.

While the church is often involved in all these endeavors, they do not define the church's mission. The maximization of operating surplus and the provision of quality educational and care services are clear goals for both corporates and not-for-profits. However, churches do not have clear counterparts to such goals, nor precise mechanisms to assess effectiveness and efficiency. Churches often have to negotiate multiple interests and demands while dealing with goal ambiguity.[14] The multiplicity of interests and demands is especially the case in churches such as the LCA that have many agencies that work across various sectors.

The objects of the LCA identify the LCA's mission. The LCA aims to fulfill the mission of the Christian church in the world by proclaiming the Word of God and administering the sacraments in accordance with the Confession of the Church.[15] As far as the LCA seeks to fulfill the Christian church's mission in the world, its mission is the church catholic's mission. The mission of the LCA and hence the church catholic seeks to take into account the church's environment while staying faithful to its purpose. In other words, as a confessional church, the LCA seeks to ensure that all that the church does, conforms to the confessions of the church,[16] which function as the church's guiding principles.

[14] Paul DiMaggio, "The relevance of organization theory to the study of religion," in *Sacred companies: Organizational aspects of religion and religious aspects of organizations*, ed. N J Demerath et al., Religion in America (New York, NY: Oxford University Press, 1998).

[15] *Constitution of the Lutheran Church of Australia Queensland District*, (Milton, Australia: Lutheran Church of Australia Queensland District, May 2010, 2010), 4.

[16] Lutheran Church of Australia Queensland District. *Short Constitution of the Lutheran Church of Australia Queensland District.*

However, the LCA lives out its confession incarnationally in the world by encouraging its congregations and agencies to carry out their mission to their local communities.[17] Its emphasis on incarnational theology gives the Lutheran tradition specific anchor points within each space and time. Lutheran theology does not confess a solely transcendent deity, far removed from the everyday events of humanity. For the Lutheran tradition, a God who does not make a difference in this life, quickly becomes a useless hypothesis.[18]

Expounding the Lutheran tradition's incarnational theology, Dietrich Bonhoeffer, the nineteenth century Lutheran theologian and clergyman whom the Nazis martyred in 1945, wrote, "God is not free of man...but for man...God is there, which is to say, not in eternal non-objectivity, but 'haveable'...'graspable'."[19] Bonhoeffer pointed out that "One of the first theological principles must continue to be that where God is, he is fully."[20] Therefore, Bonhoeffer was able to affirm the congregation as "the locus of God's reconfigured presence in the world."[21]

The Lutheran tradition's incarnational understanding of ministry is a call to understand one's environment and take seriously to present Christ to all as "haveable" and "graspable" to use Bonhoeffer's terms. Christ as "haveable" and "graspable" highlights the Lutheran Reformation maxim that the infinite reveals or holds itself in the finite – *finitum capax infiniti*.[22] This is a critical insight into how Lutheran theology understands God's presence and, therefore, the church's presence in the world.

17 Lutheran Church of Australia Queensland District. *Short Constitution of the Lutheran Church of Australia Queensland District.*

18 Depoortere, 2007, as cited in Daniel J Peterson, "Beyond deep incarnation: Rethinking Christology in radical Lutheran terms," *Dialog: A Journal of Theology* 53, no. 3 (2014).

19 Bonhoeffer, 1962, as cited in Ronald A Carson, "The motifs of 'kenosis' and 'imitatio' in the work of Dietrich Bonhoeffer, with an excursus on the 'communicatio idiomatum'," *Journal of the American Academy of Religion* 43, no. 3 (1975): 548.

20 Dietrich Bonhoeffer, *Christ the centre*, ed. Eberhard Bethge (New York, NY: Harper & Row, 1966), 100.

21 Peterson, "Beyond deep incarnation: Rethinking Christology in radical Lutheran terms," 248.

22 Kurt K Hendel, "Finitum capax infiniti: Luther's radical incarnational perspective," *Seminary Ridge Review* 10, no. 2 (2008).

The church's incarnational theology shapes the LCA as an open and not a closed system. It fundamentally seeks to, in the words of the objects of the church, "carry out its mission to its local community."[23] In essence this suggests that the LCA is created and seeks to function by interacting with its communities in seeking to achieve synergy and greater value for society. However, defining what incarnational ministry means in all the environments in which the church finds itself is not a simple exercise. Goal definition as a concept is problematic for a church. It is particularly so in an organization such as the LCA, due to being collectively governed, resulting in multiple interests.[24] How the LCA's overarching governance ensures that the multiple interests of the church's agencies do not become competing goals is a particular challenge.

The LCA as a Social Actor

The LCA is called to carry out its mission to its local communities together with all its agencies and as more than simply a collection of individuals. The word "church" is a collective noun, and from an organizational perspective, the church's action is more than the aggregation of individual people's actions. In other words, the church as a synodical complex has agency as a social actor.

Its character as a social actor comes from emergence, where "the whole becomes more than the sum of its parts... [and] the interaction of the parts of a system gives rise to new characteristics, qualities, attributes or properties, which are not inherent in the parts."[25] Because of emergence, the church has agency beyond the aggregation of its constituent parts. Hence, it can make decisions and behave as an entity of its own volition and be held accountable like any other organization.

[23] Lutheran Church of Australia Queensland District. *Short Constitution of the Lutheran Church of Australia Queensland District*, 4.

[24] DiMaggio, "The relevance of organization theory to the study of religion."

[25] Elisabeth Dostal, *Biomatrix: A systems approach to organisational and societal change*, Third Edition ed. (Cape Town: BiomatrixWeb, 2005; repr., Second Imprint 2006), 10.

Organizations are social actors not only in legal terms, but because society grants them a license to operate. Society grants that status practically and linguistically and interacts with them as an entity with unique properties.[26] Organizations, as social actors, also carry with them an inherent need for unity beyond the individual. Organizations are interested in what is beneficial to their existence and well-being, how internal competing goals can be solved and how conflict can be resolved. In other words, organizations have organizational intentionality, which is not dissimilar to the process of an individual making decisions about internal conflicts and difficult decisions, the resolution of which helps to "further articulate the self."[27]

This is not to say that an organization with agency beyond its aggregated parts cannot fracture or splinter. Indeed, paradoxically the fracturing of church organizations is well documented among churches. This is perhaps especially true for collectively governed organizations such as the LCA with complex goal definitions and multiple interests, from the local congregation or parish to education and aged-care. The goals of various entities can become competing goals in the synodical complex.

The Religiousness of Church Agencies

As Jeavons[28] points out in his seminal work into religiousness of church agencies, the diversity in organizations that are usually labeled religious is striking,

[26] Brayden G King, Teppo Felin, and David A Whetten, "Perspective—finding the organization in organizational theory: A meta-theory of the organization as a social actor," *Organization Science* 21, no. 1 (2010), https://doi.org/https://doi.org/10.1287/orsc.1090.0443.

[27] King, Felin, and Whetten, "Perspective—finding the organization in organizational theory: A meta-theory of the organization as a social actor," 297.

[28] Thomas H Jeavons, "Identifying characteristics of 'religious' organisations: An exploratory proposal," in *Sacred companies: Organizational aspects of religion and religious apsects of organizations*, ed. N J Demerath et al., Religion in America (New York, NY: Oxford University Press, 1998). And Thomas H Jeavons, "Understanding Religious Organizations: Implications and Concerns for Public Policy and Social Welfare Services" in *In search of the nonprofit sector*, ed. by Peter Frumkin and Jonathan B Imber (New York: Routledge, 2017).

from small local congregations and parishes to multimillion-dollar healthcare organizations and from elite educational institutions to ragged homeless shelters. Jeavons points to research in the United States, which reveals that many organizations with religious roots have no current religious organizational self-identity or label or anything explicitly religious in their culture, while other organizations are affiliated in name with a religious body but have no religious self-understanding.[29]

Jeavons suggests seven fundamental aspects of an organization's "religiousness," using the common substantive definition of religion from the Oxford American Dictionary, as "belief in a superhuman controlling power, especially of a God or gods...[and] the particular system of faith and worship deriving from that belief."[30] He suggests the following questions:

> First, how religious is the organisation's self-identity? Second, how religious are its participants? Third, how religious are its material resources and their resources? Fourth, how religious are its goals, products or services? Fifth, how religious are its decision-making processes? Sixth, how religious is its definition and distribution of power? Seventh, how religious are the other organisations or organisational fields with which it interacts?[31]

Jeavons' seven questions are noticeably qualitative in nature and reflect the reality that evaluating an organization's religiousness is not a specific science. The questions, however, can provide self-awareness for churches such as the LCA, which continues a gradual process of what can be called "agencification," as its congregational membership continues to decrease in-line with other mainline churches in Australia while its influence through its agencies continues to increase.

Several factors can heighten self-understanding for churches like the LCA with agencies. These factors can

29 Jeavons, "Identifying characteristics of 'religious' organisations: An exploratory proposal."

30 Jeavons, "Identifying characteristics of 'religious' organisations: An exploratory proposal," 79.

31 Jeavons, "Identifying characteristics of 'religious' organisations: An exploratory proposal," 81.

include evaluating the names which the church adopts for its agencies and the mix of people of faith in contrast to those who do not profess faith. They can also include the origin of the organization's financial resources, the product that is produced, the process of planning and who is involved, the organization's exercise of power and other partner organizations.[32]

The Dual Structures within LCA's Church Polity

In explaining churches from an organizational perspective, Chaves[33] focuses specifically on authority structures within denominations, arguing that many denominations continue to have a fundamental misunderstanding over their structure, mistakenly viewing denominational structures as unitary and not as the dual structures they often are.

A unitary view of denominational structures can also occur in a church such as the LCA. This is because the synodical complex's highest governing body is a unitary organ, the convention of synod and its board. Chaves argues that what often is not appreciated is that the one governance body oversees a dual structure, which consists of a religious authority structure and an agency structure.[34]

Chaves points out that his insights are not new in ecclesiastical organizational literature. What is new, however, is the claim that the "two structures remain essentially parallel structures, performing different kinds of tasks, responding to different parts of the environment, coping with different kinds of uncertainty, and containing separate lines of authority."[35] Up to a point this is also the case with the LCA.

32 Jeavons, "Identifying characteristics of 'religious' organisations: An exploratory proposal."

33 Mark Chaves, "Denominations as dual structures: An organizational analysis," in *Sacred companies: Organizational aspects of religion and religious aspects of organizations*, ed. N J Demerath et al., Religion in America (New York, NY: Oxford University Press, 1998). And Mark Chaves, *American Religion: Contemporary Trends*. Second ed. (New Jersey, USA: Princeton University Press, 2017).

34 Chaves, "Denominations as dual structures: An organizational analysis."

35 Chaves, "Denominations as dual structures: An organizational analysis," 175.

However, the two separate lines of authority ultimately meet at the level of the convention of synod and its board.

Chaves argues that all denominations with agencies contain a religious authority structure as one part of their dual structure, with the religious authority structure mainly concerned with compliance.[36] Compliance and control language is evident in the LCA's constitutional documents. For example, the first paragraph after the church's objects at the beginning of the LCA Queensland District's constitution uses modal verbs to define the qualifying characteristics of members,

> The membership of the District shall consist of baptised members of congregations within its assigned area which [shall]… accept and hold the Confession of the Church; [shall]…accept the Constitution and By-laws of the Church and the District; [shall]…submit a Constitution and By-laws acceptable to the Church and the District; [shall]…undertake to participate in the work of the Church and the District, and to promote their Objects.[37]

From the article on membership, the LCA Queensland District's constitution moves to discussing the qualifying characteristics of clergy and from there to the church's authority and powers:

> The District, in accordance with the provisions of the Constitution and By-laws of the Church and this Constitution, shall have authority and power to make rules and regulations for the administration of its affairs… The District shall have power to do all such things as the District may think incidental or conducive to the attainment of the Objects of the District or any of them. The jurisdiction of the District over the congregation shall, subject to this Constitution and the By-laws, include the following rights… to ensure faithful adherence to the Confession of the Church… to apply discipline when departure from the doctrine of the Church is evident…

36 Chaves, "Denominations as dual structures: An organizational analysis."

37 Lutheran Church of Australia Queensland District. *Short Constitution of the Lutheran Church of Australia Queensland District*, 5.

> to enlist wholehearted cooperation in the program approved by the Church or the District in the fulfilment of its Objects… to take action when persistent disregard of the resolutions of the Church or the District is evident.[38]

The LCA's constitution, therefore, utilizes compliance language. The main objects of compliance are congregations, parishes, clergy and congregational members. The church's agencies make a brief appearance toward the beginning of the LCA Queensland District's constitution as part of the church's objects. The constitution defines them as services for the church's members and agencies in the service of human need:

> The District accepts the Objects of the Church, and shall promote them within its assigned area. These Objects are to… establish and maintain schools and other institutions and to foster all other means whereby the members of the congregations receive Christian education…minister to human need in the name of Jesus Christ our Lord and provide institutions and agencies for this purpose.[39]

Chaves explains that 'the primary sociological difference between religious authority structures and agency structures is in their orientation to congregations...[where] the goal orientation of the religious authority structure generally is internal, while the goal orientation of the agency structure is external.'[40]

Essentially, due to their external goal orientation, the church's agencies function as an agent of the church in the world, hence the nomenclature, albeit often an agent with a clear commercial dimension. From a constitutional perspective, congregations have an accountability to the church's authority structure, even though each congregation submits voluntarily to its place in the synodical structures. Each congregation chooses to journey synodically with

[38] Lutheran Church of Australia Queensland District. *Short Constitution of the Lutheran Church of Australia Queensland District*, 7.

[39] Lutheran Church of Australia Queensland District. *Short Constitution of the Lutheran Church of Australia Queensland District*, 4.

[40] Chaves, "Denominations as dual structures: An organizational analysis," 182.

other congregations and agencies that make up the church's synodical complex.

However, for the church's agencies, if they are not meaningfully linked to the church's mission through local congregations, which are the foundational entities for the church's mission, congregations can purely become a resource. They can become a resource of funds, expertise, and personnel, among other things, and a primary market of students for church schools, residents for aged-care homes, contributors for the church's superfund and investors in the church's building society. Both the church's authority structure and the church's agency structure interact with the church's congregations, but this interaction's nature can differ as Table 1 explains.

Dimension	**Religious Authority Structure**	**Agency Structure**
Orientation toward congregations and individual members	Compliance and control	Resource or client
Goal orientation	Internal – Religious compliance and control	External – Engagement with the environment
Basis of differentiation	Geographical segmentation	Functional differentiation
Basis of legitimate authority	Synodical (vote/ consensus) and Theological (Office of the Ministry)	Synodical (vote/ consensus) and rational/legal
Primary boundary for scope of authority	Member/non-member	Employee/non-employee

Table 1 Religious Authority Structure vs. Agency Structure[41]

[41] Adapted from Chaves, "Denominations as dual structures: An organizational analysis," 183.

The basis of differentiation between the church's authority structure and the agency structure differs, as the church's authority structure segments congregations by geography into districts and zones. In contrast, the church's agencies are differentiated by function, i.e., schools, aged-care, youth ministry, early childhood services and the like. As Chaves highlights, "the principle of growth within agencies is functional differentiation, rather than geographical segmentation."[42] The basis of legitimate authority is similar for both structures since the final authority for both from an internal perspective is the church's authority structure. However, agencies need to contend with more external legal regulation.

Due to the agencies' task orientation as organizations, managers lead agencies in a very similar fashion to non-ecclesiastical organizations.[43] If a clergyperson is called to work within an LCA agency, they work under the agency's leader concerning daily tasks. However, they function under their bishop in relation to pastoral and doctrinal oversight. An agency's employees may or may not be members of the church, whereas the primary boundary for the scope of authority in the church's authority structure is not employee/non-employee, but member/non-member.

The dual structure implied above can present challenges to the church's ministry within the church's agencies, particularly with accountability and authority in areas where the church's authority structures and agency structures overlap. The overlap of the two structures can, for example, create tension and confusion concerning ecclesiastical oversight of non-ordained ministry personnel within church agencies, or the teaching of Lutheran doctrine within church schools, or the approach to contemporary ethical issues.

In regard to relying on the LCA for resources, LCA agencies have by necessity become increasingly independent from the church in recent decades. Today, the LCA's agencies

42 Chaves, "Denominations as dual structures: An organizational analysis," 183.

43 Chaves, "Denominations as dual structures: An organizational analysis."

receive the vast majority of their revenue from the state and federal government and from their clients, rather than from congregations, the district or individual parishioners. As the LCA's membership continues to decline numerically, church agencies rely less on congregations for clients. Hence, they have had to become competent in marketing their services to society at large.

This drift away from congregations by church agencies has been dictated by external circumstances rather than by design. However, it requires skillful governance and management by both the church's authority structures and executive directors of church agencies. In particular this is necessary in that the church and its agencies do not succumb to internal secularization. Internal secularization occurs and leads to decreasing control that religious authority has over its agencies and their organizational resources; hence, secularization is most accurately defined as the decreasing scope of religious authority.[44]

The threat of internal secularization is reduced in the LCA since the final authority over the entire church, including its agencies, is the convention of synod. Also, in regard to the LCA as a legal entity, the General Church Board and the various District Church Boards are charged with ensuring "that the program and policies of the Church are carried out."[45] The LCA's by-laws for the districts also place the district bishop into an oversight role as the district's chief administrative officer, including all church bodies and auxiliaries.[46]

Chaves argues that when denominational agencies are run by executives who are progressively independent of the denomination's authority structure, the organizational changes that follow are correctly understood as internal secularization, although it does not mean that internal secularization is a linear, inevitable process that follows

[44] Mark Chaves, "Intraorganizational power and internal secularization in protestant denominations," *American Journal of Sociology* 99, no. 1 (1993).

[45] *Lutheran Church of Australia Queensland District by-laws part A,* (Lutheran Church of Australia Queensland District, November 2015, 2015), 13.

[46] Lutheran Church of Australia Queensland District. *Short Lutheran Church of Australia Queensland District by-laws part A.*

increasing independence from the church.[47] This is where Jeavons' seven aspects of an organization's religiousness [48] can help the LCA and other mainline churches in Australia to measure the level of internal secularizations that their agencies may have.

Australian Churches as Not-for-Profit Service Providers

Many organizations in the not-for-profit sector in Australia are governed by churches, which creates an additional layer of governance complexity and accountability. Of all the Australian Charities and Not-for-profits Commission registered charities, religious organizations form the largest category, with some research suggesting that twenty-three out of the largest twenty-five community service organizations have religious beginnings.[49]

While not-for-profit organizations are heterogeneous, they're all organizations that are barred from distributing their surpluses. A 2010 Productivity Commission report into the not-for-profit sector in Australia found more than 600,000 not-for-profits in Australia, with approximately 440,000 being small community groups, while around 60,000 were 'economically significant.'[50] Fueled mainly by government funding, registered charities reported $142.8 billion in annual revenue in 2017, employing over one million paid employees.[51] In 2014, the sector reported having over five million volunteers.[52] The volunteers' equivalent wage value in 2012-13 was $17.3 billion.[53]

47 Chaves, "Denominations as dual structures: An organizational analysis."

48 Jeavons, "Identifying characteristics of 'religious' organisations: An exploratory proposal."

49 Lucas & Robinson, 2010, as cited in Nicholas Aroney and Matthew Turnour, "Charities are the new constitutional law frontier," *Melbourne University Law Review* 41, no. 2 (2017).

50 Productivity Commission, Contribution of the not-for-profit sector: Productivity Commission research report, XXVI (Melbourne, Australia: Commonwealth of Australia, 2010).

51 Aroney and Turnour, "Charities are the new constitutional law frontier."

52 Pro Bono Australia, *State of the not-for-profit sector: Survey*, Pro Bono Australia (Windsor, Australia: Pro Bono Australia, 2014), https://probonoaustralia.com.au/wp-content/uploads/2016/01/pdf_survey_2014.pdf.

53 Aroney and Turnour, "Charities are the new constitutional law frontier."

While government funding has increased, the need for critical scholarship into churches and not-for-profit organizations has also increased, especially concerning the new welfare regime's governance implications.[54] A lingering absence of empirical data concerning not-for-profit governance, limits academic observations about the sector's governance. The sector is still suffering from insufficient empirical data from a large, representative study.[55]

While the not-for-profit sector provides a significant contribution to Australia's economic and social landscape, a recent study into the sector found that one in three respondents who work in the sector, believes that Australian not-for-profit organizations are not well-run.[56] The study also pointed out that 63 percent of not-for-profit organizations have difficulty retaining good staff, 76 percent of respondents said the critical issue affecting their organization's effectiveness was poor board composition and only 14 percent believed that the sector invests adequately in itself.[57]

The report highlights a sector that is struggling to manage its growth adequately, as its role in delivering government-funded services continues to grow. As the sector grew in the 1970s and the 1980s, many not-for-profit organizations found government contracts a significant funding source. This enabled substantial capacity growth in the sector. Still, as the organizations grew, there was further pressure to grow even larger, resulting in many Australian not-for-profit organizations being locked into growth, fearing

54 Catherine McDonald and Greg Marston, "Patterns of governance: The curious case of non-profit community services in Australia," Article, *Social Policy & Administration* 36, no. 4 (2002).

55 Francie Ostrower and Melissa M Stone, "Moving governance research forward: A contingency-based framework and data application," *Nonprofit and Voluntary Sector Quarterly* 39, no. 5 (2010), https://doi.org/https://doi.org/10.1177/0899764009338962.

56 Good Foundations, *The foundations of a well-run not-for-profit - Why internal investment is critical: 2017 survey results*, Good Foundations (Balmain, Australia: Good Foundations, 2017), https://static1.squarespace.com/static/540bee12e4b0566ddac6613c/t/59a711d6cf81e045cfb46261/1504121315484/2017Survey_Report.pdf.

57 Good Foundations, *The foundations of a well-run not-for-profit - Why internal investment is critical: 2017 survey results*.

that if they didn't grow, they'd be discriminated against and lose government contracts.[58]

Before the government funding-induced growth of the sector, Australian not-for-profits were mainly small organizations working cooperatively with other not-for-profits, without competition.[59] Since the introduction of contracting of government services to the sector, organizations have had to guard their competitive advantage over other organizations in the same fashion as for-profit corporations. Hence, the Australian government's policy reform into its service delivery has had a direct influence in introducing competitiveness into Australia's not-for-profit sector.

This has, in turn, added growing pressures for not-for-profits to become more professional and to integrate corporate governance principles into their structures, focusing more on skill-based governance rather than community participation and representation.[60] In this new and emerging context, not-for-profits have had to re-evaluate their original calling to govern their organizations as agents of community, based on shared values, while operating as agents of the government.

An example of this tension was contracting employment services to the not-for-profit sector through the government's Job Network program. Before being renamed Job Services Australia by Australia's federal government in 2009, not-for-profit organizations administered approximately 50 percent of the program.[61] Qualitative analysis of the not-for-profit sector's involvement in the Job Network program has high-

[58] Mark Considine, Siobhan O'Sullivan, and Phuc Nguyen, "Governance, boards of directors and the impact of contracting on not-for-profit organizations: An Australian study," *Social Policy & Administration* 48, no. 2 (2014), https://doi.org/https://doi.org/10.1111/spol.12055.

[59] Considine, O'Sullivan, and Nguyen, "Governance, boards of directors and the impact of contracting on not-for-profit organizations: An Australian study."

[60] Considine, O'Sullivan, and Nguyen, "Governance, boards of directors and the impact of contracting on not-for-profit organizations: An Australian study."

[61] Colette Rogers, "The impact of the Australian government job network contracting on not-for-profit service providers," *Australian Journal of Public Administration* 66, no. 4 (2007), https://doi.org/https://doi.org/10.1111/j.1467-8500.2007.00552.x.

lighted conflicts between contractual obligations toward the government and the not-for-profits' values and mission.[62]

A Productivity Commission report into the Job Network program highlighted conflicts between compliance and rating systems of the program and the values and mission of especially not-for-profits governed by religious-based organizations. Mission Australia, for example, highlighted in its submission to the Productivity Commission's review that focusing heavily on outcomes as influenced by the program's rating system resulted in organizations having to force appropriate recordable results at the clients' expense.[63]

In its submission to the review, the Salvation Army also highlighted the conflict between the organization's mission and values and the government's bureaucratic requirements on not-for-profit organizations, pointing out that such conditions undermined the Salvation Army's key focus of helping to improve the options of unemployed people.[64] As a response to the Commonwealth's 2005 proposal to significantly increase penalties if the unemployed failed to comply, the Salvation Army argued that "suspending welfare benefits was inconsistent with Christian justice."[65]

The Roman Catholic Church's St. Laurence Community Services estimated that 50 percent of an employment consultant's time was taken up in administrative and compliance activities.[66] This added pressure to priorities those job seekers who were most likely to find jobs rather than those in the greatest need of support. One staff member noted in a research report of the program that "there are simply not enough hours in the day, to push everyone to achieve their best, and the most job ready, have to be given priority."[67]

62 Rogers, "The impact of the Australian government job network contracting on not-for-profit service providers."

63 Productivity Commission, *Independent review of the job network*, Commonwealth of Australia (Canberra, Australia: Commonwealth of Australia, 2002), https://www.pc.gov.au/inquiries/completed/job-network/report/jobnetwork.pdf.

64 Productivity Commission, *Independent review of the job network*.

65 Murphy, "Church and state in the history of Australian welfare," 265.

66 Productivity Commission, *Independent review of the job network*.

67 Greg Marston and Catherine McDonald, *The front-line of welfare to work: The implications of radical reform in Australia*, School of Social

In particular, the Job Network Program highlighted the necessity for churches to review their place as welfare and educational providers for government services. The need to evaluate their involvement from a holistic, mission and faith perspective became acute as governmental demands on faith-based service providers increased. Faith-based service providers needed to consider the conditions under which they were willing to act for the government in providing welfare and educational services, being aware of mission drift and whether areas such as compliance and efficiency inherently changed the nature and ethos of a church agency.[68]

Balancing Stakeholder Interests

While the government is often the biggest single funding provider for church welfare agencies, the church, together with the not-for-profit sector in general, needs to juggle several stakeholders' interests. The balancing of stakeholder interests has been identified as one of the significant challenges of not-for-profit governance.[69] In a recent study into Australian not-for-profits, the government was identified as the most significant single funding source for the organizations that took part in the research, contributing on average nearly half of the participating organizations' income, with another 25 percent of revenue coming from service fees.[70]

While organizations surveyed indicated that their most significant single funding source was the government, the government came in at a third place in their response to the organization's most important stakeholders, with the most important stakeholder group being their clients,

Work and Applied Human Sciences, The University of Queensland (Brisbane, Australia: The University of Queensland, 2006), 8, https://www.researchgate.net/publication/242235251_The_Front-line_of_welfare_to_work_The_implications_of_radical_reform_in_Australia/citation/download.

[68] Murphy, "Church and state in the history of Australian welfare."

[69] John Chelliah, Martijn Boersma, and Alice Klettner, "Governance challenges for not-for-profit organisations: Empirical evidence in support of a contingency approach," *Contemporary Management Research* 12, no. 1 (2016), https://doi.org/https://doi.org/10.7903/cmr.14538.

[70] Chelliah, Boersma, and Klettner, "Governance challenges for not-for-profit organisations: Empirical evidence in support of a contingency approach."

followed by employees.[71] According to the 2010 Productivity Commission's research report, approximately 33 percent of funding for economically significant not-for-profits came from the government and about 50 percent from internal funding, such as fees for service.[72] These organizations have more capacity to generate income from services compared with smaller not-for-profits.

Hence, for both smaller and larger not-for-profits, government funding is a significant source of income, resulting in not-for-profit boards having to balance multiple stakeholders' interests.[73] Lyons points out that due to their distinctive characteristics, not-for-profit organizations do not have clarity to whom they are accountable, "to members, financial backers, to users of services, or to religious figures in the case of church organizations."[74]

While recipients of services are a priority stakeholder group for not-for-profits, research reveals the problematic nature of Australia's not-for-profits' funding dynamics, where the government is often the largest donor, while recipients of services are identified as the most important stakeholders.[75] The Job Network example highlights the struggle that many church owned not-for-profits can have between contractual obligations toward the government and the not-for-profits' values and mission to assist society's most needy from a faith perspective.

The introduction of contracting government services via churches to the community has impacted the church's self-understanding. It has forced many church-run institutions and, hence, the church, to guard their competitive advantage

71 Chelliah, Boersma, and Klettner, "Governance challenges for not-for-profit organisations: Empirical evidence in support of a contingency approach."

72 Productivity Commission, Short Contribution of the not-for-profit sector: Productivity Commission research report.

73 Chelliah, Boersma, and Klettner, "Governance challenges for not-for-profit organisations: Empirical evidence in support of a contingency approach."

74 Lyons, 2001, as cited in Rogers, "The impact of the Australian government job network contracting on not-for-profit service providers," 398.

75 Chelliah, Boersma, and Klettner, "Governance challenges for not-for-profit organisations: Empirical evidence in support of a contingency approach."

over other organizations in the same fashion as for-profit corporations. Consequently, the Australian government's policy reform over recent decades into its service delivery, has introduced competitiveness into the church and church-run institutions. The church inevitably becomes more corporate in its outlook as it competes with other organizations for government-funded contracts. This by necessity shifts the church's focus away from its members to focus on organizational stakeholders.

The growth of LCA's agencies has continued, while the Christian church's place as a whole in Australia continues to change and as parishes and congregations continue to decline numerically. The LCA's shrinking congregational base and growing agency base presents the LCA with fundamental questions. Is the LCA primarily a gathering of congregations with agencies to aid and further the church's missional work? Or is the LCA primarily an entity with growing agencies with a reducing number of congregations supporting the work of church agencies? The Lutheran church's ecclesiology strongly indicates the former, while a rapidly changing place in the Australian public space puts pressure on the church to conform to the latter. The question, however, is not unique to the LCA but is timely and relevant for many other mainline churches in Australia.

The Australian Church's Changing Landscape

The place of the Christian church in the Australian public space continues to change. People are focusing less and less on the church as a place for social meaning and deeper significance. This can be seen for example, by the trend to discard church weddings and funerals, with over half of funerals and 70 percent of weddings in 2016 being conducted by civil celebrants.[76]

The Australian Lutheran church's place also continues to change in step with the rest of the Christian church. As Bishop Emeritus Greg Pietsch reported in his final report as bishop to convention of synod of the Lutheran Church of Australia Victoria and Tasmania District in 2016, much has

76 Greg Pietsch, "Reflections on the status of the church as we look towards the future," *Lutheran Theological Journal* 52, no. 1 (2018).

changed in the way that the LCA engages its communities from the beginnings of Lutheranism in Australia:

> Our congregations, and the communities to which we hope to take the gospel, are much changed from their beginnings and in most cases from the years we might look back to as the 'best.' But going back to the past won't cut it. For most of our history we have planted new congregations by following Lutherans as they spread out across the land, or by finding them as they came from overseas. That mission strategy is largely over. Now our 'going' is of other kinds, even though the One we go with is unchanged. We have much to learn, beginning with ourselves.[77]

From the perspective of the ongoing decline in church attendance and membership, the Christian church in Australia faces significant shifts in how it is included in the Australian social narrative. The challenges to the Christian church in Australia are significant and cannot be underestimated. The 2016 Australian Bureau of Statistics *Census of Population and Housing* painted a grim picture of the Christian church's receding influence in Australia. Although the percentage of Australians identifying as having no religion has steadily increased since the first census in 1911, the rate of Australians identifying as having no religion significantly increased from 2006 to 2016, from 19 percent, to 30 percent. The most significant increase was between 2011 and 2016, when an additional 2.2 million Australians reported having no religion.[78]

While the Australian national narrative has always included a notion of irreligiosity and irreverence, the Christian church has held an important place in the formation of the nation and its most influential institutions. The Christian church's narrative is intertwined in the history of Australia from colonial times onwards. It is also notable

[77] Pietsch, "Reflections on the status of the church as we look towards the future," 15.

[78] Australian Bureau of Statistics, *2016 census data summary: Religion in Australia* (2016), https://www.abs.gov.au/ausstats/abs@.nsf/Lookup/by%20Subject/2071.0~2016~Main%20Features~Religion%20Data%20Summary~70.

that there is wide acceptance of the Christian church's close relationship with the state by providing governmental services by church-run institutions.

While the separation of church and state regularly features as a topic of conversation in the public space, this has never been a firmly entrenched separation like it is in the United States. For example, this is demonstrated by the use of religious oaths, church functions and services for the legal profession and regular prayers in parliament.[79] From the early days of white settlement, Christianity has been a foundational element of Australian society, although this has been carried lightly and with measured amounts of larrikin-like irreverence. As Hudson points out,

> Thousands of churches were built and tens of thousands of men and women gave their lives to religious concerns, often at personal cost, not only in cities but also in country towns...In Australia there was sometimes no rigid divide between the religious and the secular. Whereas Americans take the separation of church and state for granted, Australians have largely accepted government help for religious institutions and, despite the shift away from religious education in the 1870s, they have made extensive use of church schools and hospitals.[80]

Conclusion: Church Agencies as Mission Entities

As an operator of significant aged-care, community service and educational agencies that receive state and federal government funding, the LCA finds itself in an increasingly complex regulatory operating environment. This is especially problematic due to an elevated level of competition from other not-for-profit and for-profit agencies. This coincides with considerable shifts in the Christian church's place in Australia's national space. Church attendance and membership continue to decline. However, the size and number of many of LCA's agencies continue to grow. This has

[79] Wayne Hudson, *Australian religious thought* (Clayton, Australia: Monash University Publishing, 2016).

[80] Hudson, *Australian religious thought*, XIII, XV.

resulted in a church that is decreasing in membership and worship attendance, governing agencies that are increasing in size, governance, and management complexity.

From a theological perspective, however, the LCA is well placed to respond to the governance challenges that the changing landscape presents since Lutheran ecclesiology allows for a contingency based governance architecture. Because Lutheran ecclesiology is incarnational, it takes seriously the call to understand the church's environment and respond in a way that engages communities with the gospel. This is why the LCA and its agencies exist and it is the purpose out of which flow the church's mission.

The LCA, therefore, must ensure that the church's governance processes and structures are fit for purpose in all of the church's expressions. The LCA needs to design its governance processes and structures to be fit for the purpose and mission of the church and not change its purpose and mission to fit the church's governance. In other words, governance processes and structures need to be designed and developed based on the church's purpose and mission, not based on an inherited or pre-determined structure. This is especially so since Lutheran theology does not predetermine the church's ecclesiastical structure, but is contingency based.

It must do this, however, remembering that in Lutheran ecclesiology, the church does not exist without the preaching of the gospel in accordance with Scripture and the administration of the sacraments according to the gospel. Everything that the church does, whether through congregations, parishes, or church agencies, needs to relate back to this foundational understanding of the church in the Lutheran tradition.

Traditionally, LCA agency leaders have had a clear understanding why their agencies exist and their role in the mission of the church. LCA agencies are legitimate agencies of the gospel in their communities. This is a significant strength of LCA agencies and institutional leaders. In the future, however, as the regulatory environment of church agencies continue to grow in their complexity and as the LCA struggles to identify future institutional leaders from among its members, the LCA has to be mindful that this does not change.

If the LCA isn't able to fulfill its mission through its agencies, it cannot change its purpose to fit the agency, nor can it simply ignore its purpose. In that case, the LCA has no other option but to divest the agency, because all that the church does is to be based on its purpose to fulfill the mission of the Christian church in the world by proclaiming the Word of God and administering the sacraments in accordance with the Confession of the Church.

Church Polity: International Studies in Protestant Church Polity
Autumn 2021 2(1), pp. 67-86

BOOK REVIEW ESSAY

Leon van den Broeke and Allan J. Janssen (eds.), *A Collegial Bishop Revisited: Classis and Presbytery At Issue*, (Kampen: Summum Academic, 2020), Deddens Kerkrecht Serie / Deddens Church Polity Series, vol. 4, 148 pp (ISBN: 9789492701145)

The publication at hand is the result of a conference held on 22-23 May 2018 about Classis and Presbytery at the Theologische Universiteit Kampen in the Netherlands. The organisers were also responsible for a previous international conference on the same theme held at the New Brunswick Theological Seminary in the United States of America in 2008. This publication, though, consists of seven academic articles. These articles are preceded by a Preface and an Introduction but also by an In memoriam to Allan Jay Janssen (1948-2020), which was written by coeditor Leon van den Broeke. Allen was a much-appreciated participant at several conferences of *inter alia* the International Reformed Theological Institute and Church Polity congresses. It is appropriate that Allen had the opportunity to write the Afterword for this publication.

Van den Broeke states the actuality of the publication by referring to a remark by one of the attendees: "The classis is more under pressure than I thought." (p. 19). He provides the following (personal) observation: "Not only because of the increasing depreciation of the classis and the presbytery, but also because of the depreciation and decreasing knowledge among office-bearers of church polity in general and the misunderstanding of what it is, ought to be and the consequences for all the general assemblies, like the classis and the presbytery." (19). The book is not a plea for "putting church polity in the spotlights ... It is about the theological understanding of the church as it manifests, or ought to manifest (regional) catholicity." The book is structured around the following question: "But how can the classis or the presbytery manifest regional catholicity?" (p. 21). Subthemes addressed by the different authors include inter alia the classis and authority, *koinōnia* (fellowship), the (new) context of the classis and the presbytery, and some historical aspects of the development of the classis and the presbytery.

But first, the central question of the book has a practical tenor. Van den Broeke elaborates: "Catholicity requires an answer to the difficult question how office-bearers and/or the local churches overcome and live with their differences." (p.21). This book seeks to find a solution for the classis or presbytery to manifest catholicity on a regional level. This approach attempts to contribute to the adequate structuring of the different articles within the theme and sub-themes of the book. This is a strength of the publication—and despite some typing errors, repetitions of words and other technical problems that occur in some places, it contributes to a sound publication. The practical approach makes it also possible to state (and even compare) the classis and presbytery's realisation of catholicity on a functional level. Yet, one should not expect a church polity comparison between the classis and the presbytery regarding the origin, nature and function as each developed within two recognised and established church polity traditions in the reformed branch of the sixteenth century Reformation, namely the presbyterial and the presbyterian traditions. However, the practical approach of this book brings the administrative and bureaucratic nature of contemporary classis and presbytery ("managerial bodies") to the fore (p. 25).

Yet, because of this practical approach, the strength of the publication is the honest formulation of contemporary problems of classis and presbytery and some related issues in the context of a specific church community, which, though recognisable by the readers in their own context, indicates problems experienced by most reformed church communities over the world. The first part of this review focuses on the article's responses to and elaborations on the core question. Second, a few remarks are made as seen from the broader framework of reformed church polity focusing on the theme of the book under discussion.

Allan J. Janssen addresses the theme, "Who Says? The Authority of the Classis/Presbytery in a Reformed Church." The basis of his argument is that all authority comes from God. "Granted that original, and final, authority comes from God and God's self-revelation, authority comes in different guises." The authority *of* the church and *within* the church is, according to Janssen, a relative authority. He expresses the main interest of the article as follows: "Ministers of the Word have an authority to proclaim the Word to a congregation and to administer the sacraments. *Governing authority is of a different kind*; it has to do with leading the church in such a way that the church conforms to what it is meant to be, a gestalte of the kingdom of God. And that is what primarily is in focus in this paper how this 'relative' authority is distributed among the offices, assemblies, congregations and church members." (My emphasis - JS). Under the sub-theme "A church reformed," a short perspective on the nature of the church is given. Janssen bases his overview mainly on the Heidelberg Catechism (p. 28-30). He emphasises the following: the church as a creation of God, the work of the Son as He gathers and protects his church through Word and Spirit (creatura Verbi), the importance of the proclamation (ministry) of the Word, and the Reformed believers understanding of the anti-hierarchical character of the church. (Why the latter is indicated in the past tense, is not entirely clear.) However, the point Janssen makes, is that "theologically, it is the freedom of the Word to form the church in each locality–the Word proclaimed in both preaching and sacrament." Janssen sees a relationship between the freedom of the Word and the first article of the church order of Emden 1571. "Hence the famous first article of the church order of Emden: "No church shall have precedence or rule over another, no minister over minister, no elder over elder, no deacon over deacon, but rather each will be alert for all suspicion thereof and occasion thereto." Under the sub-theme "Episcopal authority," he argues that the Reformed-minded developed a system of assemblies, wherein they were cautious to allot the authority carefully over and against the hierarchical polity of the Roman Catholic Church. (p. 30). The main question posed in this regard is how the authority is then distributed between the classes and the General Synod? (p. 30). Janssen answers this question on a functional level by rendering the different mandates allocated to the different assemblies.

"What has evolved is a parliamentary process whereby a simple majority 'discerns' the will of God for the church!" Under the sub-theme "Problems," Janssen states the problem of the allocation of specific authorities to the different church meetings. But what should the churches do when a church council or a classis, e.g., clearly acts against the doctrine and the synod agrees with the complainants, but states that it is not within the authority of synod to direct boards of elders on the matter, or to intervene so that the authority allocated to synod does not allow any intervention with the specific classis? Janssen does not suggest an answer to the question but mentions that the Standards of Unity to which churches adhere, only "work so long it works" (p. 35). Many churches in the reformed tradition will recognise the problem which Janssen states in their own church communities. There is no question about the actuality of this contribution.

Leon van den Broeke asks the question "For What Reason is the Classis on Earth? The Classis as a Buffer between Ecclesial Individualism and Regional Catholicity in the Context of Globalization, Regionalism and Globalization." The article focuses on church polity developments in the Protestant Church in the Netherlands (PCN) by making use of aspects of the renewal project, which was accepted by the PCN, namely Kerk 2025. It is divided into five sub-themes. The first is Kerk 25 and the classis. Under this sub-theme Van den Broeke refers to a statement of a former secretary-general of the general synod of the PCN, Arjan Plaisier. After Plaisier had considered five societal developments important for the (development of the) church, he stated that "too much time and energy in the church is devoted to governance, and not to following Jesus" (p. 39). The nature of the reorganization of the PCN was to embrace simplicity, space, and transparency. Simplicity meant that there should be fewer procedures, rules, regulations and less focus on the institution of the church. Space meant that the church should yield more to the local church and fresh expressions of church (the so-called *pioniersplekken*). Here van den Broeke provides the golden thread which gives his reflections in his conclusion and connects the different sub-themes of the article. He states: "The nature of his reorganization was: simplicity, space, and transparency, *but was more ecclesial than ecclesiological in nature; it is more the outcome of an ecclesial reflection than the result of a profound theological reflection about the nature of the church* (ecclesiology)." (p. 39, 50, my emphasis; JS). Van den Broeke states that all this emphasizes the fact that the nature of the classis since 2018 is considered more as fellowship and a platform than as supervision. He concludes that the PCN makes too much of a distinction between supervision and fellowship "as if fellowship can only be reached without supervision, and as if supervision excludes fellowship." (p. 42).

Under the sub-theme "An ecclesiological buffer," Van den Broeke states that the classis acts as a buffer between independentism on the one hand and synodocracy on the other. In this sense the classis acts to prevent too big a discrepancy between the different local churches, but also the church on a national level. "Moreover the notion of the classis is important to safeguard the catholicity of the church in the region. The local churches and their consistories need each other, can help each other and assist one another." (p. 43). The sub-theme "Mobility," indicates how the development of the railway system in the Netherlands (1839-1939) changed the concept of space and enabled churches to be present at the classis venue and contributed "to the notion of the classis as an ecclesial regional entity" (p. 44). It includes a discussion of "mental distance," which indicates that "ecclesiastical scaling up tends to lead not only to a geographical, but far more a mental distance, let alone a spiritual distance with view to (delegated office-bearers of consistories of) other congregations and the notion of regional catholicity" (p. 50)

Under "For what reason is the Netherlands on earth?," Van den Broeke describes six virtues and characteristics of the Dutch mentality. These virtues are observed from a study about the so-called polder landscape of the Netherlands. It entails the following: safety, equality, material things, freedom, honesty, and attention. Armies and Navies discusses the nature of the Dutch nation as a naval rather than a marine nation. The distinction is taken from the philosopher Haroon Sheikh. It intends to show that a nation can be considered like either an army, e.g., a nation connected to a territory, or as a nation like the Dutch who can be considered as a "navy." These nations are regarded as "more entrepreneurial, individualistic and cosmopolitan in nature" (p. 46). The last two sub-themes mentioned above find an application in the sub-theme "For what reason is the classis on earth?" It especially considers the virtues developed in the Polders as a possible application to classis and church. Van den Broeke states: "The people in the polder needed each other to protect themselves against the floods. This notion is absent in a theological constellation where there is no emergency requiring people to work together. The threat of disaster is absent" (p. 48). Furthermore, "The classis can hardly be considered as a natural, sociological entity" (p. 48). However, local churches are expected to take care of one another, look after one another, and avoid the temptation of individualism. (p. 50). In his conclusion Van den Broeke then continues that on the one hand there is "... a secular society, individual choices, a network society, digital revolution, and globalization. On the other hand the reorganization of the classis structure seems to be more the result of ecclesial than of ecclesiological reflection" (p. 50). Because this article reflects on a church community's ideal of an internal renewal and its process, the more "inquisitive" remarks may result in its condemnation too, which the "collegial" dustbin church communities sometimes reserve for awkward and even unwanted questions and remarks. It would be a shame!

An ecclesial approach to church, to make use of Van den Broeke's term, usually leads to a church community stumbling over and against its self-erected structures; the (valid) accusation is sometimes made that irrespective of the church's ideal of de-institutionalisation that it again lapses into the maintenance of its own processes and structures. To keep structures and processes intact requires work and before long even more processes. And what about the kingdom of God in an ecclesial approach to church? This article goes to the core of the PCN's view of church and may even question the fundamental assumptions about church in its renewal document.

Klaas-Willem de Jong writes about the theme, "Half a bishop: A Critical Outline of the So-Called *Classispredikant* in the PCN," which indicates that May and June 2018, the first ministers to become a so-called *classispredikant* were elected and called. The term *classispredikant* was accepted with a large majority. However, the description of the *classispredikant* relates closest to the known office of the bishop. But the term, "bishop," was not acceptable because of its historical baggage, which included *inter alia* the idea of a church hierarchy. De Jong does the following: he provides an outline of the position of the *classispredikant* in the PCN, discusses theological developments in the PCN which re-evaluates the bishop and a bishop-like office, gives an examination of the office of the moderator in the United Reformed Church (URC) in the United Kingdom, and evaluates this new position in the PCN. He also formulates an answer to the research question, namely, to what extent the *classispredikant* can be called a bishop. (p. 56). De Jong refers to three PhD studies authored by Eddy van der Borght (2000), Margriet Gosker (2000), and Hans Kronenburg (2003). These authors are all in support of the office of a presbyter (p. 57). De Jong gives a balanced critique of the work of Kronenburg and indicates why he makes use of the profile Kronenburg provides. "I will use Kronenburg's profile because it reflects the essentials mentioned in the BEM report and it is the only detailed and well-substantiated profile tailored to the Dutch Protestant context" (p. 59). He then discusses The practical need for a bishop-like office or officer. He indicates five points.

First it became difficult to find delegates for classes meetings and some meetings rarely even reached a quorum. Second, there was a shortage in office-bearers to fulfill specialized tasks like visitation. Churches, in fact, also did not see the relevance of something like a practice of visitation. In this sense, visitation should be revitalised within the churches. It seems that the *classispredikant* will therefore have the responsibility to visit congregations less frequently but with a qualified purpose (visitation). Third, there already was in two of the predecessor churches of the PCN, a concern for the pastoral well-being of the office-bearers. One of the functions of the *classispredikant* is to act as a *pastor pastorum* to ministers in their often demanding and insecure positions. However, in terms of the Church 2025 project, the care of ministers is to be made concrete only as a part of measures to improve the mobility of the ministers. The *classispredikant* is responsible for raising the issue of mobility from time-to-time in the classis. (p. 60-61).

Fourthly, in a missionary context with missionary challenges the *classispredikant* represents the church and acts as the face of the church in the specific region. Fifthly, previous ways of dealing with conflict and discipline seem insufficient. It may be that the *classispredikant* can act more quickly and more effectively in a situation. De Jong also addresses the point that the classis is not only important for *episkopē*, but for *koinōnia*. He also describes how the *koinōnia* will find expression in the bigger classes. The *theological motives* which De Jong indicates (already under his discussion of Kronenburg's contribution) are four motives to support the introduction of an episcopal ministry: a pastoral motive (response to the need for 'leadership with a human face'), an ecclesiological motive (a bridge 'between unity and pluriformity,' local and national church, authority and management), an ecumenical motive and a cultural (or missionary) motive" (p. 57-59). Furthermore: "With exception of the representative task, the responsibilities ascribed to him or her not only belonged to the responsibilities of the classis but remain, for the function of the *classispredikant* is principally embedded in the classis" (p. 62). In the comparison with the moderator in the URC, De Jong states that the *classispredikant* has a less independent position and has less authority in comparison to the moderator.

The above-mentioned comparison serves as a basis for the answer he formulates regarding the central question: "Despite the acknowledgment by other denominations of the *classispredikant* as a bishop, according to the current PCN regulations he is at most half a bishop; however, he does have the potential to develop into an almost whole one" (p.68). De Jong gives a thoughtful explanation of the PCN's acceptance of a "half" bishop. I have read Van der Broght's dissertation, to which De Jong refers, but do not find the argument convincing. The key question, however, is as follows: The catholicity of the church does not find expression in a person, but in the common creed and confession and believers' mutual recognition of each other on the basis thereof. How is the relationship between the doctrine of the church and the life of the church maintained in the development of the *classispredikant*?

In Kathleen S. Smith's theme: "Balancing Tensions and Encouraging Health: The Classis Renewal Movement in the Christian Reformed Church in North America," Smith states that the understanding of the classis as *episkopē* and as *koinōnia* is also operative in the CRCNA. Her article focuses on a description of how the classis in the CRCNA functions, what the historic and currently-changing ecclesiastical vision for the classis is, and how it relates to the leadership of the denomination. She also indicates how the CRCNA balances tensions between different understandings of classis. According to Smith it seems that CRCNA lean toward the view that the classis has authority only as delegated to it by the churches, and very little hierarchical authority. She also states that focus of classes seems to change. Previously the focus was on the execution of a list of items that the churches had to check on their credentials to ensure they were performing their duties properly. Today the classes focus on requests for help and engage in the discussion of ministry issues. It seems, therefore, that a change, that can be described as a move from a focus on *episkopē* to *koinōnia* is taking place. A result of this shift is that the classis is acting more like a church! However, there is a movement within the churches to change the appeal procedure. It entails that a classis will have the authority to appeal against a decision of another classis, according to Smith, exercising in this way an authority of *episkopē* over the relevant classes. This process of change is however still not finalised. She concludes with the remark that the classes of the CRCNA are leaning toward the *koinōnia* understanding of the classis in their practices and may continue to do so under a new definition of the classis, if adopted by Synod 2019." (see p. 73-82).

Adam Csukás's theme is about "Classis in the Evangelical Church of Czech Brethren." He gives an interesting and necessary historical overview of the Evangelical Church of Czech Brethren (ECCB), which is, outside a small circle mostly in Europe, not known to many church historians and church polity scholars. He states that the church polity of the ECCB is undoubtedly 'presbyterial-synodical' in the sense of German and Hungarian Protestant church polity. However, he also indicates similarities between the development in the PCN acceptance of the *classispredikant* and the *senior* or the Synodal *Senior* in the ECCB, which was introduced in 2018 (p.85-102).

Joseph D. Small writes about "How Polity Dies: Form without Substance in the Presbyterian Church (USA)." Small states that the American Presbyterianism's form of government which provided a model for the American government, is a fable. However, this previously well-accepted fable has lost its appeal. The demythologising of the myth has the flip side, according Small, that it enabled Presbyterians to avoid recognition of "the ways in which the American political system's disfunction shapes and reinforces the current practice of Presbyterian polity" (p. 103). For Small this is indicative of a disillusioned position of church polity. "In the church's life throughout time and place, preserving and transmitting apostolic faith, proclaiming the gospel and celebrating the sacraments, shaping public and personal righteousness, and coordinating mission in and to the world have never happened automatically. Communion in the faith and communion among the faithful require patterned relationships, and so Christian community requires structured ecclesial life. Church order is not a peripheral concern, but a central ecclesiological matter" (p. 104). In this article Small focuses on the existential problem faced by American Presbyterian polity: "that its own chosen and carefully crafted democratic procedures are being drained of their substance.... The church's existential problem is less about democratic procedure itself than the underlying norms that make democratic procedure possible" (p. 106). He then discusses the different themes, "How Democracies Die," "The Waning of Mutual Tolerance," "The Waning of Institutional Forbearance," "The Death of Polity," "Presbyterian *Episkopē* and the Good of the Church," "Continuity in Apostolic Faith," "Unity of Life," "Bearing Witness to the Gospel," and "Reconstructing Guardrails." Small describes mutual tolerance and institutional forbearance as guardrails necessary to the proper functioning of Presbyterian polity (p. 108 ff; 110 ff). However, it will not be reinstated by resolutions encouraging or requiring them. "It will take more than critique of their absence and urging their renewal to bring about a return to 'life together'" (p. 112). Small states that the starting point is renewed attention to what polity itself is intended to accomplish. It is indicative that the purposes of *episkopē*–oversight–especially the *episkopē* exercised by presbyteries, must be rediscovered. It may be of key-concern, "leading to reform of sessions on the one hand, and the general assembly on the other" (p.112). Small comes to the following conclusion (Reconstructing Guardrails):

> Continuity in apostolic faith, unity of life, and witness to the gospel are not programmatic initiatives generating competing goals, strategies, and tactics, leading to proposals that are submitted to votes. They are the ongoing responsibilities of *episkopē*. The church's councils–sessions, presbyteries, synods, and the general assembly–can be liberated from captivity to the strictures of parliamentary procedure, set free for *koinōnia* in the grace of the Lord Jesus Christ, the love of God, and the communion of the Holy Spirit. Repair of the organizational guardrails of mutual tolerance and institutional forbearance is not the prerequisite, however. Serious, sustained attention to the faith, centered on Scripture, prayer, focused theological work, and sacraments will generate a quality of faithful life together in which mu-

tuality and forbearance are once again as natural as breathing. (p. 117)

Small puts his finger on a major problem of contemporary reformed/presbyterian church polity. There seems to be a discrepancy in many church communities about the relationship between the theological content on the one hand, and the church polity process or rather church government on the other hand. But what is the theological content, which must be provided to see to a true church process? Small gives a description of some of the fundamental premises necessary to inform and even protect democracy. In this process *episkopē* can, according to Small, play an important role. But is the revitalization of "church democracy" an answer to provide theological content to the church process?

John P. Chalmers views the "Presbytery as the Engine of the Church." His contribution gives an awareness to the complex history of the emergence of Presbyterian government as the dominant force in Scottish religious life. However, he also explores ways in which the classis or the presbytery itself might recover some of its original potency and its role as a *bishop* in the church. He states the pious ideal of the classis and the presbytery; their business was 'to seek first the Kingdom of heaven' (Matthew 6:33) (p. 123). Chalmers then states a continuing awareness throughout all the contributions in the *Collegial Bishop*, namely that the churches paid a high price for the way in which classis and presbytery have been allowed to be overtaken by legal, bureaucratic, disciplinary and ceremonial functions. He states the following aspects of presbytery life and culture, namely that it is more often more competitive than supportive, more often concerned with discipline than with compassion, more often driven by law than grace, more focused on getting through the business than on stopping to pray. For Chalmers the most serious question is if our presbyteries are willing to be at the forefront of the change which is required in our church life?

"Because the purpose of God is not about saving denominations or institutions from extinction; the purpose of God and the mission of church is about building communities of justice and peace and love – our presbyteries can be a part of that mission or they can drift into irrelevance and obscurity" (p. 128). He further elaborates on the central function of the presbytery in its relationship to the General Presbytery and the Kirk session to indicate the centrality and importance of the presbytery. "Presbyterianism already has a mid-engine structure, we just have to give that engine the fuel it needs and it could be the engine of change and the engine of the church" (p. 132). Chalmers states that presbytery can provide the wrap around for churches to operate and succeed like bees in a beehive. Bees cannot survive as individuals. According to Chalmers the presbytery provides for the situation where "no person has to work alone, no minister is unsupported, no one person has to be an expert in every discipline, as well as being accountable to one another, [and] people are responsible for one another." (p. 130).

It brings us to the second part of this review. The aim is to give a few comments out of the broader framework of reformed church polity focused on *Collegial Bishop*. I do not intent to provide answers to the questions post be the different authors, but rather ask where we should start to address these questions. But first things first.

I want to start with a general remark: the impression from the first pages of the book expressing a point of view that keeps worrying the reader. Throughout the book there is strong focus on the context and what it demands of church polity (cf. De Jong). Yet, as mentioned above, the problems indicated in the different articles are mostly the result of a functional approach to the church and church polity. The references to theology and church history are, with few exceptions, quite informative but not fundamental. In this regard it may also be mentioned that it seems unsettling that throughout the book it is not clear what either reformed or presbyterian church polity entails and what the differences between these different systems of classis and presbytery are. Why bother to mention both historically-accepted and independent church politic systems within the reformed branch when they are essentially considered as synonyms? A practical approach to church polity should be welcomed, but why not make a clear distinction within the ambit of the discipline? Church Polity can refer to the (encyclopaedic) theological science responsible for determining the principles for the government of the church and formulating it in a specific order, while church government (which should not be confused with cybernetics) refers to the government of the church (the church order and its application). *The Collegial Bishop* may therefore be seen as a church politic publication with the focus on church government. The Dutch theologian, Bram van de Beek, once mentioned that church polity is not only a *kombuiswetenskap* ("kitchen science"), but a theological science developed and practised from behind the desk in the study. It indicates that reformed church polity is not only a practical science concerned with e.g., internal processes and procedures of churches, but that the doctrine and the discipline of the church are integrated and have theological-historically developed together. In fact, the doctrine (*doctrina*) of the church calls for its practical embodiment in the discipline (*disciplina*), and the latter embraces the doctrine to implement (or rather minister) the belief to the edification and expansion of the church.

A mere practical approach may in the context of contemporary church and church polity beg the question: Are Church Polity and Practical Theology drinking from the same fountain, by which any aspect of the church, theology or the environment within which the church finds itself can become the object of theology (church law) as long as the theologian has the intention to serve the church with it?[1] Dirk de Vos[2] mentioned that this may be a threat for church polity within the confines of the PCN. Yet which church community in our time is excluded from this pitfall? And then too, church polity cannot be a stranger to the context. Reformed church polity is theology.[3] This premise is fundamental to the development of church polity. Church polity can fundamentally have no other focus than Reformed theology. Therefore, reformed church polity scholars should recognize

1 Cf. W.D. Jonker, *In diens van die Woord* (Pretoria: NG Boekhandel Transvaal, 1981), p. 20.

2 D. de Vos, *Hervormd en gereformeerd kerkrecht: Een vergelijking* (Kampen: Brevier Uitgeverij, 2017), p. 566

3 This point is well-established in the literature and in the practice of the Reformed tradition in South Africa.

that the study of church polity is primarily about the Word of God. In this review "reformed" church polity indicates the development of church polity in Calvin's Geneva as it was further developed in South Africa under the Dutch influence. The question should in my view be what church polity provides *in* and *for* the church in its context, rather than the other way around. Church polity should not get caught up in a notion of a "theology of interest" or even a contemporary "contextual" theology. External factors like the context, the law, political process, etc., should not determine the nature of church polity. I focus further in this review on some of the lasting features of reformed church polity with a specific focus on some of the ongoing themes in the *Collegial Bishop.*

The reformed tradition, more than other church politic traditions, acquired from the sixteenth century Reformation an affinity with the government of Christ over his church. Ample theological reasons may be provided as a motivation for the latter, but it mostly centres in the reformed concept of church: in this the soteriological aspect of the salvation in Christ is never rejected or even diminished but serves as the basis for and even incorporates the reformed view of sanctification. Where the church in Luther's view can rather be observed around the marks of the church, the Reformed-minded developed the idea of the church as a commonwealth. Yet how is it perceived in reality in the world? The reformed-minded saw in Scripture an order for the calling and edification (which informs and inspires the mission) of the church. In summary: The church is the new order or the new dispensation that finds expression in this world. This new community, the body of Christ (*corpus Christi*), comes into existence because of the order God provides for the church. In the literature this order is sometimes indicated as an order of the Word, an order of the Holy Spirit, or an order of the proclamation of the Word of God: The effect of the proclamation of the kingdom results in the creation of the church. The body of Christ lives by the order of the proclamation of the Word by called office-bearers. Calvin[4] at one stage says that God held humans in such high esteem, that God engaged them in His work, though he could

4 Cf. Institutes, IV.3.1.

do everything himself. On this basis reformed church polity never had an affinity to the German schism between church and law. Through the proclamation of the Word the church (believers) is called by Christ, edified and equipped to fulfill its mandate in church and society. Of course, there is also a focus on the believers and the relationship between the church offices and the believers, but the reformed focus is on the office.

(i) The extensive focus in all the articles on the institutional aspect of the classes and presbytery in the *Collegial Bishop* exemplifies the question of what should theologically and historically be understood as reformed church polity (cf. René de Reuver, p.15). The focus in the early reformed Reformation was on the reformation of the office, and even more specifically on the function of the office-bearers, and not on a possible status or position of a person. The development of the church meetings did not change this approach. The focus was on the meeting (classis) as a gathering or an assembly (*'n verzameling*) of local churches. It merely indicates that the local churches came together. The classis, however, was the most important gathering of the different local churches but the early church orders—at least until the synod of Dordrecht 1618/19—do not describe classis as an institute or a body. It provides stipulations for the delegates to fulfill their mandate under the guidance of the Word. In fact, these church orders put the emphasis on the place of the Word in the church and the ministry of the Word in the different situations. The church government of the reformed (which includes the function of *episkopē* as it finds expression in the *Collegial Bishop*), especially that of Calvin, was pastoral in nature. This is consistent with the intent of ecclesiastical oversight and government. Both do not have a legalistic nature but give expression to a father's love for a child, but which the child must admonish. The church government does not work with coercion, it does not threaten and does not blackmail, but is patient in persuading the person by means of the ministry of the Word.

The idea of the classis or a church meeting as an institute, a legal entity or a synodical system did not exist in the early era of the reformed Reformation (cf. Afterword by Janssen, p. 135 ff.). Instead of institutionalising the church meetings, the institutional aspect of church according to the reformed view found expression in the local church: that is under the proclamation of the Word and the ministry of the sacraments. There the citizens of the kingdom of God are already visible in this dispensation. Would that be the directions to take for the de-bureaucratization of church meetings. Why should the classis in any case be a body to experience the Christian *koinonia*? (cf. Van den Broeke). The use of the term "reformed" in the *Collegial Bishop* can, in my view, not find support in the early reformed Reformation of the sixteenth century.

(ii) The development of the so-called reformed Orthodoxy brought about many of the themes which find expression in the *Collegial Bishop*. However, I do not contest that the Orthodoxy was reformed, but rather that it should be acknowledged as a unique expression of the reformed faith in a specific era where, for example, the influence of rationalism, etc., decisively influenced aspects of reformed church polity. Church polity was influenced by the development of the Puritans in England and to an extent also by the *Nadere Reformasie*, a concomitant movement in the Netherlands. The church polity of the reformed Orthodoxy found expression *inter alia* in the development of impressive synodical structures of the church. One may think in this regard of the work of Charles Hodge, but also that of Gijsbert Voetius in the Netherlands. Voetius's interest in the church was, in the first place, not determined from a church politic (theological) premise, but in the juridical definition and allocation of authority to different church meetings. The influence of his views cannot be underestimated, because the so-called *Doliantie-Kerkrecht* of F.L. Rutgers, H. Bouwman, Joh Jansen and others, at the beginning of the twentieth century was mainly a systematization of the work of Voetius. It provided for a strong juridical approach to reformed church polity over and beyond the pastoral approach of the early reformed Reformation.

Later in history there were some major developments and influences on reformed church polity in the Netherlands, *inter alia* the development of the Dutch Collegialism, etc. It seems, however, that the historical origin for many of the themes and problems presented in the *Collegial Bishop* may possibly find their origin rather in reformed Orthodoxy and not in the reformed Reformation.

(iii) On this basis I would suggest that the question is not which authority is on a functional level allocated to the different church meetings (Janssen). According to the reformed view the church meetings have the same authority. The authority vests in the Word of God. Yet, church meetings provide the opportunity for the delegates (i.e., office-bearers) through the discernment of matters by considering the Word, to decide on the different issues. The Church Order of Dordt 1618/19 refers in several instances to "more churches." It does not indicate the establishment of a hierarchical system, but refers to the gathering of more persons, which means more gifts, more insight and wisdom for the adjudication of certain matters. The visitation is therefore not per se an episcopal function of the classis but an arrangement by the classis to enable office-bearers to fulfill their mandate. Moreover, the questions asked, according to article 44 (DCO) are a function of the delegates between themselves and not the classis as in institute executing a form of supervision over the churches. As such the advice given by a classis (DCO, Art. 41) is a way in which the churches exercise their commitment to mutual support, etc. It certainly is an expression of *koinonia* (cf. Smith).

(iv) The point of departure of Reformed ecclesiology is not the church, but the proclamation of the kingdom of God. The church cannot involve the kingdom in the execution of its mandate. The church is the fruit of the proclamation of the kingdom. Is there possibly a new freedom for the church to escape from its self-erected structures of the so-called institutional church? Or to acknowledge the institutional aspects of the local church and to treat the church meetings as true meetings which dissolve after such a meeting—the only evidence of its existence being the notes of the meeting which serve in the churches? After all, Christ gives the *charismata* of office-bearers in the local church, where it finds expression in the ministry (as services).

(v) Democracy in our society is without a doubt a valid and preferable system of state government (Small). After the church, however, developed mutual tolerance and institutional forbearance as premises for a successful democratic society, a new institutional structure or a missiological program remained the same as assignment of the church: You must love each other (We must love one another). Love remains the norm of reformed church polity; no democratic process or parliamentary procedure can inspire or convince a person to love their neighbor: only the government of Christ through his Word and Spirit changes the hearts of people. Isn't there a fundamental shift in our understanding of our polity do not and cannot anymore, because of our church structure, appeal to the Christian love as the foundation for our relationships?

A Collegial Bishop Revisited: Classis and Presbytery at Issue is a valuable contribution to orient church and theology about the problem which contemporary classis and presbytery experience to give expression to the catholicity of the church. There are no easy and short answers to the questions posed in the different contributions. I hope that this review may contribute to the continuation of a much needed discussion.

Johannes Smit
North-West University, South Africa
johannes.smit@nwu.ac.za

BOOK REVIEW

Trimargono M. Ebenheser, *Interfaith Marriage: A Study of Contextual Church Polity in the Religiously Plural Context of Indonesia* (Zurich: LIT Verlag, 2020). Ecumenism and Church Polity: Global Perspectives, 322pp (ISBN: 9783643913371)

This work is a dissertation defended at the Protestant Theological University in the Netherlands, with Prof. Dr. Leo J. Koffeman as supervisor and Prof. Dr. Gerrit Singgih as co-supervisor. The Rev. Dr. Trimargono M. Ebenheser is a pastor serving at the Sidomukti Javanese Christian Church (GKJ) in Salatiga, Indonesia.

The focus of this study is interfaith marriage, a complicated and delicate issue faced by churches in Indonesia due to the diversity among the churches themselves, the national context of religious pluralism, and problematic marriage laws and regulations. This study is a theological research in the field of church polity as a theological discipline (p. 15) (Indeed, church polity is theology!). Against this background, Dr. Ebenheser develops theological principles regarding interfaith marriage by employing a dialectical and critical dialogue of actual cases and concrete experiences concerning interfaith marriage with the foundational message of the Bible, relevant Christian faith traditions and theological perspectives.

His thesis statement is that "... interfaith marriage, which is actually a concrete reality in a pluralistic society, exists as a natural thing [p.287], ... is a legitimate, Christian marriage. God is intimately involved in the intimate partnership of the couple. The involvement of God in the covenant of marriage happens when spouses consent and commit themselves to create a life of equal and intimate partnership in loyal and steady love. This is the point from which we construct the theological understanding of interfaith marriage [p. 292]." To come to his thesis, he took the following academic steps.

First of all, a thorough review was carried out on the civil law system on marriage in Indonesia, which is one of the causes of the complexity of interfaith marriage problems. The Marriage Law No. 1/1974 neither prohibits nor permits interfaith marriage. As a result, its implementation relies entirely on the Civil Registry Offices in Indonesia, which generally do not allow interfaith marriage. This was reinforced by the decision of the Constitutional Court in 2014 which rejected the petition to amend Article 2.1. of the Marriage Law No. 1/1974 in order that interfaith marriage can be implemented in Indonesia. Then, the Civil Administration Law No. 23/2006 is seen as providing new hope for the implementation of interfaith marriage. However, it depends on the theological and ecclesiastical positions taken by the churches in Indonesia, which in reality do not share the same opinions regarding interfaith marriage.

The dissimilarity of theological and ecclesiastical opinions of the churches in Indonesia is discussed in the next chapter. The author makes an in-depth analysis of five churches in Indonesia, namely the Batak Protestant Christian Church (HKBP), the Protestant Church in Western Indonesia (GPIB), the Protestant Christian Church in Bali (GKPB), the Indonesian Christian Church (GKI) and the Christian Churches of Java (GKJ). These churches are not seen as representing all Protestant churches in Indonesia, but are offered as examples. The survey was carried out by looking at their historical backgrounds, biblical bases, and church teachings, both as historical heritage and contemporary views. In conclusion, churches in Indonesia are divided roughly into two groups, namely those who accept and those who do not accept interfaith marriage. Of course, there are also some who position themselves somewhere in between.

At the end of his research, the author develops contextual theological principles in church polity for churches in Indonesia. To begin with, the author presents understandings of marriage from Catholic, Lutheran, Calvinist and Dutch Protestant traditions. Moving on from there, two basic theological frameworks are used to develop theological principles in church polity. The first is the biblical interpretive framework to obtain a basic theological understanding of interfaith marriage. Through interpretations of several key texts, from both the Old and New Testaments, it turns out that there is no single biblical view on interfaith marriage. However, it is shown that the issue of interfaith marriage has been faced and struggled with by faith communities described in the Bible in their respective social-religious contexts. The second theological framework is taken from the systematic theology of SW Ariarajah, which the author connects to the results of the research held by the Communion of Churches in Indonesia (PGI) in 2013 described in the previous chapter. The conclusion of the study confirms the openness of churches in Indonesia to the concept of pluralism and their commitment to inter-religious dialogue. This openness is then seen as an ecclesiastical and social resource that should be optimally employed. Therefore, Ariarajah's theological concept of hospitality, which focuses on dialogue among religious people to embrace one another, is seen as suitable and effective to develop a more open view of interfaith marriage. However, the descriptions of the theology of the family and theology of marriage in this part are seemingly misplaced. The two basic theological views should properly be integrated in the sub-section "The Theological Basis of Marriage" in the previous section. All in all, in this broad perspective, the author conclusively states that interfaith marriage is a legitimate form of Christian marriage.

Through this study of church polity, the author does not intend to invite churches in Indonesia to simply follow his theological-ecclesiastical views. Church polity is a theological discipline that studies and develops theological principles that can be considered for use by churches in formulating their church order in their own ecclesiastical realm as part of their identity. This dissertation has succeeded in contributing such theological principles on the issue of interfaith marriage and the main thesis is a valuable basic point of view. From here, the author encourages churches in Indonesia to explore and formulate their own basic theological-ecclesiastical views in their own historical backgrounds and contexts. Then, it is hoped that the churches will be enabled to formulate and/or revise their church order to be a concrete, effective tool of service in dealing with the problem of interfaith marriage.

In general, this dissertation enriches the theological literature in the field of church polity, both in Indonesia and internationally. The basic scheme is clear, but the descriptions in certain sections that are more detailed often require a lot of effort for us to be able to follow and understand them well. In Indonesia, this work needs to be read and studied by churches, academics, theologians, and especially church members, whether or not they have directly encountered the issue of interfaith marriage. This book should even be read by wider circles of people from different backgrounds and contexts, because, as expressed by the author, "Interfaith marriage is a means [for all parties concerned] to be able to promote peace and to ennoble humanity in a religiously plural society" (p.266).

Lazarus H. Purwanto
Jakarta Theological Seminary, Indonesia
lazarus.purwanto@gmail.com

Made in the USA
Monee, IL
04 November 2026

67386608R00056